That's Opera

That's Opera

200 Years of Italian Music

Edited by Gabriele Dotto

Prestel
Munich · Berlin · London · New York

RICORDI
a Bertelsmann company

PRELUDE · Plácido Domingo/*My Life and Opera*

My life has been dedicated to music and especially to opera. It is therefore only natural that I should be pleased to contribute these few words for such an important occasion as the commemorative exhibit for the bicentennial of the Ricordi Historical Archive.

I have always loved Italian opera, and the possessions of Ricordi & C.'s Archive constitute an extremely valuable and variegated collection of material representing a golden epoch in the history of this musical genre. I am thinking particularly of 19th-century opera, which has provided me with many of the roles I have interpreted over the course of my career. It is quite an extraordinary world, one which is capable like no other of conciliating rarefied cultural nuance with a fundamental quest for broad public appeal. Literature and cinema have sometimes been successful in this venture, but opera best embodies the interracial, intercultural, intergenerational dream of being able to combine communication and inquiry, general sentiment and profound personal reflection, immediate impact and the more long-term, accumulated effects of time. Unfortunately, that which normally strikes forcefully at the heart often slips into trivial, commonplace terms; just as that which lends subtle and refined contours to human thought and endeavor is just as often lost to the general public. But opera, whether old or new, has always overcome this challenge. The most inspired music can penetrate everyday life with primordial, one might almost say atavistic energy, bringing millions of people "into tune with" the composer, the performer, and other listeners while losing nothing of its structural complexity in the process.

Opera is a world of its own that continues to attract both young and old. One need only observe how audiences fill the theaters not only for the standard favorite classics by Rossini, Verdi, and Puccini, but also for operas by Baroque and contemporary composers, testimonial that the roots of opera reach back well before the 19th century and that it continues to bear significant fruit today with outstandingly successful world premières.

I am truly happy, therefore, that that this exhibit will help draw an ever greater public to the marvelous patrimony of opera, to a genre that defies the pre-established flow of "official" time by replacing it with the temporal measures of music and memory. An aria by Verdi can render an instant eternal, just as we are beginning to learn from the latest scientific discoveries regarding the rapport between time and space. An aria can bring the action to a halt in order to explore a feeling, an emotion, a thought, or even a circumstance. It can draw our emotions from deep memory by means of images and dreams. "Real" time is in fact operatic time, that same discontinuous sense of time which is common to us all. When I am on the stage, interpreting characters that come alive with every performance in a kind of endless temporal loop, I surrender to this sensation. I try to control it when I conduct but it always takes on a life of its own, imposing instead an opposite logical direction indicated by the creative designs of the composer. Opera is well suited to withstand the ever-growing tendency to neutralize things, to anesthetize the effects of pain and pleasure, to chase blindly after possessions for a tomorrow that never arrives. Opera can trigger a memory just as children do: it takes no more than a *ritornello*, a *da capo* aria for the music to return, to make us realize that we need not move mechanically forward. It also shows us that time lived by others can become interwoven with our own, like a Rossinian ensemble. And if we do not realize this then we are hardly living at all.

Music can therefore enlighten us in matters of peace, tolerance, and constructive debate through the popular narratives of opera. It teaches us that our enjoyment comes from being able to merge and grow along with others, to distract ourselves from our problems so that we can learn how to confront them and resolve them without falling prey to conflict and confusion. This is why I believe that the format chosen here for presenting the history of Italian opera in terms of selected past and present masterworks is best. Instead of simply compiling lists or quantifying descriptions of operas (exactly the kind of information that can be easily obtained about nearly everything anymore thanks to the Internet), the exhibit focuses on a few titles in order to engage enthusiasts and experts alike in exploring the actual creative process. For the first time one can follow step by step as the composer's earliest ideas evolve into the definitive score. This is even more significant in light of the fact that opera necessarily involves different artistic dimensions, making it the essence of collaboration—first among the publisher, composer, and librettist, then among publisher, composer, director, set designer, conductor, singers, and the entire theatrical staff—without which the opera could not survive. I invite the reader to embark upon this adventurous journey through the birth, growth, and enduring life of an opera, written yesterday or today.

I am grateful to opera for making me what I am. And I am grateful to opera for what it can give and will continue to give to everyone as its memory lives on in eternity.

It is no accident that a musical opera is the only kind of *opera* or work to have taken full possession of the term, embracing fundamental elements that are also common to literature, painting, sculpture, etc. When we say "opera" we refer to music. Today opera has touched the sensitive nerve of contemporary communication, opening up to a variety of cultures, genres, forms, and mediums. This means abandoning the ivory towers of the disdainful elite who create their own self-serving conceptual castles (often using impenetrable language to hide the emptiness within), but it also means avoiding eclecticism and pastiche as an easy means of stupefaction that hypnotizes the general public but refuses to recognize any sense of collective cultural identity based on inquiry, maturity, refinement, and structural rigor. The boundary between these two areas is becoming ever more difficult to define in terms that are flexible but firm, so that it can accommodate movement and open-minded debate without disappearing in the process. I do not believe there is any other artistic genre than opera, with its history past and present, that can better assist us in this ongoing quest to preserve a cultural legacy that defends us from the pernicious temptations of prosaic uniformity and commercialization.

Thus our best wishes that Italian music, with its distinguished history, continues to nurture and sustain its highest expression of genuine popular culture.

Plácido Domingo/*tenor, conductor, and administrator*

PRELUDE · Letizia Moratti

In bringing the curtain down on the celebrations for the bicentennial of the foundation of Casa Ricordi—and in the course of a journey that will last from November 2008 to 2015, the year that sees the inauguration of the Milan Expo—the exhibition *That's Opera* will bring the city's incomparable musical tradition to many of the world's major centers—Brussels, Beijing, Berlin, New York, St. Petersburg, Paris, and London.

Of international scope, the exhibition conducts visitors through every phase in the staging of a grand opera, through librettos, music manuscripts, sketches, and set and costume designs from Ricordi & C.'s Historical Archive. It affords a perfect opportunity to memorialize Giovanni Ricordi and the music publishing house he founded, which has become the stuff of legend, a symbol of musical culture and of Italian civilization.

The bicentennial festivities, which kicked off in 2006 with the exhibition *Celeste Aida* at the Teatro alla Scala that displayed for the first time the autograph score of Giuseppe Verdi's *Aida*, continue with this travelling event that is sure to enhance the international profile of Ricordi & C.'s Historical Archive, a collection of documents of inestimable value for the history of Italian music and theater.

Milan is gearing up for Expo 2015 by emphasizing a unique cultural heritage that stems from an ancient but enduringly relevant tradition capable at once of offering fresh stimuli and of attracting a diverse public from all corners of the globe.

Letizia Moratti/*Mayor of Milano*

PRELUDE · Maurizio Fallace

The initiatives undertaken by the Comitato Nazionale del Bicentenario della Fondazione di Casa Ricordi (1808–2008) over the course the bicentenary celebrations have highlighted the priceless historical and musical value of one of the most important collections of musical material in the world.

Ricordi & C.'s Historical Archive, the largest of its kind for music in Italy, comprises autograph scores by the most famous Italian composers (of opera above all) from the 19th and 20th centuries, the correspondence relating to them, and a vast performance and production collection, comprising over 10,000 original set and costume designs prepared for prestigious premières, such as Verdi's *Otello* and *Falstaff* and Puccini's *La bohème* and *Tosca*.

The exceptional value of the archive derives from the variety of documents it houses: 3,593 manuscript scores from the 18th to the early 20th century (of which 2,246 are autograph scores), some 15,000 letters from musicians and librettists, more than 10,000 set and costume designs, over 9,000 librettos and 4,000 period photos, as well as a number of Art Nouveau posters by masters of the graphic arts. It contains moreover twenty-three original scores of the twenty-eight operas written by Verdi, nearly all those by Puccini (with the sole exception of *La rondine*), and many other operas and instrumental compositions by, among others, Rossini, Bellini, Donizetti, Paganini, Liszt, Respighi, Malipiero, Casella, Pizzetti, Nono, Maderna, Donatoni.

The exhibition *Celeste Aida* (15 November 2006 to 31 January 2007), conceived and organized in collaboration with the Teatro alla Scala, the Ministry of Fine Arts (Ministero per i Beni e le Attività Culturali), and the Culture Arm (Assessorato alla Cultura) of the city of Milan, marked a successful launch for the Ricordi bicentenary celebrations and displayed in public for the first time the autograph of Giuseppe Verdi's *Aida*, which premièred at the Cairo opera house on 24 December 1871.

The goal of creating such a high-profile international cultural project could only have been realized thanks to significant backing from various public and private bodies and institutions, together with notable figures from the world of culture. The result is a vast program of exhibitions, musical events, and multimedia publications which the Direzione Generale per i Beni Librari, gli Istituti Culturali ed il Diritto d'Autore has promoted by making available new navigational tools employing interactive digital technologies which allow users to explore the texts and the context in which a given opera was composed (the "Internet Culturale" portal).

· **PRELUDE** ·

Maurizio Fallace

The diverse holdings of Ricordi & C.'s Historical Archive represent a unique resource with which to experiment a new approach to musical research, by pooling various types of documents (autograph scores, letters, visual materials, etc.). The digitalization of Casa Ricordi's Historical Archive now conserved in the Biblioteca Braidense in Milan has involved scanning autograph manuscripts of music by Verdi and Puccini and incorporating the full range of associated materials, comprising librettos, set and costume designs, sketches, staging plans, photographs, letters, and other documents that offer a wealth of information concerning the creative genesis of these operas and their staging.

The events presented under the aegis of the celebrations for the bicentenary of the foundation of Casa Ricordi culminate in the exhibition *That's Opera*, an international showcase that affords yet another opportunity to experience the publisher's artistic and musical importance in cultural history both in Italy and abroad.

Maurizio Fallace/*Director General of the Department of Library Collections, Cultural Institutes, and Intellectual Property*

PRELUDE · Tino Cennamo/*A Great Dream Becomes a Reality*

When in 1998 I took up the post of chairman of Casa Ricordi, besides the obvious intention of wanting to maintain the preeminence of the most famous Italian music publisher I was suddenly struck with an idea: Why not launch a project of international scope in celebration of its upcoming bicentennial? Though my enthusiasm led me to entertain ambitious and far-reaching ideas, at the time I broached the concept of an international exhibition on Casa Ricordi and Italian opera to my superiors and colleagues I could never have imagined that the project would take on such impressive proportions. In the context of the celebrations of Ricordi's bicentennial, and with respect to its ongoing history, the international exhibition *That's Opera* affords an ideal opportunity to underscore not only the publisher's legendary musical vocation, but also its important contribution to the art of music throughout the world.

The Ricordi imprint is internationally renowned thanks to its extraordinary composers and their wonderful operas. And naturally enough, opera, one of the supreme expressions of Italian culture, constitutes the heart of the present exhibition. Since the spread of music—and hence of its appreciation—has never been held back by national borders, the backdrop to this exhibition is naturally universal. Thus the title *That's Opera* is particularly significant: in any part of the world, one need only mention the word to stimulate interest, raise curiosity, and stir the emotions.

To turn such an event into a reality required a highly professional international team able to select and to most effectively highlight material from Ricordi & C.'s extraordinary Historical Archive, the world's largest private music archive, a unique collection housed in the glorious Biblioteca Braidense of Milan. The archive's holdings, comprising manuscript scores, librettos, set designs, costume sketches, letters, and photographs, preserves and documents two hundred years of the firm's history. A monument to the past, it is rooted in the highest musical art—indifferent to the passing of the years and immune to the vicissitudes of fashion—and has hence succeeded in conserving its cohesion and preeminent status.

That's Opera confirms that an exhibition can simultaneously delight, educate, and entertain a broad range of visitors, from opera buffs to music lovers in general, to school students and to the merely inquisitive. It is dedicated to all those who adore music and who want to explore the "making of" the complex musical experience that is opera. This is not just an exhibition: it is a unique experience, in which visitors are invited behind the scenes at a major opera production to follow step by step the fascinating process that allows a literary idea (the libretto) to be put to music (the score) and so become a fully-fledged spectacle (the opera).

· PRELUDE ·

Tino Cennamo

In its bicentennial year Ricordi represents a glorious presence that has remained an indisputable leader through two centuries of activity in an ever-changing and often turbulent field. It was in 1808 that the musician and music copyist Giovanni Ricordi, in what was a perfect amalgam of artistic awareness and acute business sense, set about writing one of the finest chapters in the history of music publishing. In this sense, Giovanni Ricordi represents a genuine high point and remains a glowing example to all: his acumen and industry could reach full fruition thanks to the stimulating and effervescent atmosphere of the Milan of his time, which was passing through what was certainly one of the most exciting periods in the city's history.

The Ricordi firm, which was established, expanded, and managed for nearly 120 years by four generations of the family (Giovanni, Tito I, Giulio, and Tito II), was subsequently guided by managers and entrepreneurs who began diversifying its activities in response to the development of new formats and media. It would be unjust, in fact, to reduce the activities of Ricordi to classical music alone, since other genres, including operetta, Neapolitan song, pop music, and contemporary music also form part of its activity. Its remarkable and internationally recognized position is today further consolidated by contemporary composers who have added and indeed continue to add to the publisher's grand heritage. In 1994, the multinational corporation Bertelsmann relaunched the Ricordi brand onto the international market, positioning it competitively and creating the conditions for its sustainable development over the coming years.

The creation of the exhibition *That's Opera* has been made possible thanks to the constructive participation of many public and private groups and institutions, and to the collaboration of important personalities from the worlds of art, culture, business, and management, all united in pursuing the common objective of a project of international impact.

The Italian Ministero dei Beni Culturali and Direzione dei Beni Librari have supported the project from the beginning, underwriting a collaboration with Ricordi that started with the housing of its collections in the Biblioteca Braidense and which is now being pursued through Ricordi & C.'s Historical Archive digitalization program promoted with the full backing by the Comitato per le Celebrazioni del Bicentenario Ricordi.

The city of Milan promoted a policy of synergic and steady collaboration with Ricordi designed to enhance not only its musical heritage but also the growth of the surrounding regional economy, the spread of enterprise culture, and Milan's image in the world.

The Department for the Superintendancy of Cultural Heritage for the region of Lombardy, an important source of support for the preservation and maintenance of the Historical Archive, was of invaluable assistance in the selection of material appearing in this exhibition.

Special thanks must go to Bertelsmann which, with unparalleled earnestness and commitment, has made this exhibition possible and which has, in conserving the materials of the Ricordi Historical Archive and in backing various strategic initiatives, demonstrated its unflagging determination to keep the name of the glorious Italian publishing house alive.

In conclusion, I shall be so bold as to quote Arrigo Boito's famous phrase "A great dream has become a reality" written when the great Giuseppe Verdi handed over the last part of *Otello* to Ricordi, thus drawing down the curtain on an idea that Boito had cherished his entire life: to measure his art with that of Shakespeare, whom Verdi called the "master of the human heart."

With pride and passion, it is still this sense of engagement and challenge that remains the guiding spirit even today for Ricordi's every undertaking. The exhibition *That's Opera* is certainly a brave venture, an incredible dream which, now that it has become a reality, is sure to remain etched in memory for many years to some.

Tino Cennamo/*Vice President and Managing Director, Ricordi & C. SpA*

PRELUDE · *Hartmut Ostrowski*

From Verdi's *Aida* to Puccini's *Tosca*, the masterpieces of 19th-century Italian opera have lost none of their irresistible attraction—not even after 200 years. On the contrary, to this day we cheer and suffer along with their tragic heroes, enjoy their famous arias, and hold the singers who perform them on the world's stages in high esteem.

But how are these compositions made? How do the brilliant artists work, without whose boundless creative powers these operas would never have been seen or heard? And what was the role played by publishers, who like composers are a fixture in European music history, perhaps more behind the scenes but just as vital? The exhibition *That's Opera* supported by Bertelsmann, aims to shed light on these aspects. We seek out the genesis of the compositions which continue to inspire us to this day, and which remain inseparably bound with the culture, and perhaps even with the identity of Italy.

The title of the exhibition—*That's Opera*—can be taken quite literally: Ricordi *is* Italian opera—the name stands for close ties with almost all major Italian composers from Gioachino Rossini, Giuseppe Verdi, and Giacomo Puccini to 20th-century contemporaries like Luigi Nono and Luciano Berio. This cultural achievement deserves our full respect and has great importance to this day, as is evidenced not least in the valuable holdings of Ricordi & C.'s Historical Archive. It goes without saying for us that this collection of scores, correspondence, stage and costume designs, and photos, arguably one of the most famous music collections in the world, is an Italian cultural heritage which requires special protection. Bertelsmann is aware of this responsibility and will ensure it is met.

Casa Ricordi and its remarkable legacy have been part of Bertelsmann since 1994. As early as the 19th century, the imprint was doing business on an international scale, and later developed into Italy's foremost music company. Today, the Ricordi "brand" is once again of primary interest for Bertelsmann—a brand whose particular splendor lies in the tradition it embodies.

All national and company differences aside, there are striking parallels between Ricordi's 200-year history and Bertelsmann's own history, which is just a quarter-century shorter. Our company values—partnership, creativity, entrepreneurship, and social responsibility—are almost identical to those in Ricordi's history. The origins of both houses lie in the printing business—the companies' founders (and contemporaries) Giovanni Ricordi (1785–1853) and Carl Bertelsmann (1791–1850) were both printers. Both houses were heavily influenced by their families Bertelsmann/

Mohn and Ricordi, which worked away for many decades in publishing and media businesses, each in different national markets but with equal passion and responsibility. Both companies experienced a tremendous international expansion in the latter decades of the 20th century, which ultimately led to their meeting in the global markets of the music industry.

We are delighted by this opportunity to introduce the visitors of this exhibition to the treasures of the Ricordi company by exploring this significant chapter in the history of European opera.

Hartmut Ostrowski/*CEO of Bertelsmann AG*

PRELUDE · Thomas Rabe

The Bertelsmann media company, 200 years of Ricordi—and an exhibition. How are they all connected? When Bertelsmann acquired the Milan-based publishing house Ricordi in 1994, it marked the beginning of a strong partnership between Europe's biggest media company and one of the largest and most culturally valuable musical archives in the world.

This connection continues today and is expanding further. Conscious of the collection's unique heritage, the archive remained part of Bertelsmann and a separate Italian company has been set up to manage it. Since then Ricordi & C. SpA, owner of the Ricordi brand and the archive, has devoted itself under managing director Tino Cennamo to the tradition of the Ricordi imprint, the preservation of valuable archive material, and the positioning of the Ricordi brand.

It is our sincere wish that this legacy continue to be treated responsibly and carefully maintained, in order to preserve its authenticity and character so closely connected with Italian culture and musical history. By supporting this international traveling exhibition, which for the first time opens up the archive and its precious treasures to the public around the world, our company demonstrates its fundamental position: to act responsibly wherever we do business.

A global media company based in Germany and an Italian music archive of international importance are closely related in today's world of music: soon after they were written, operas by Gioachino Rossini, Gaetano Donizetti, Giuseppe Verdi, and Giacomo Puccini were as well-known internationally as the hits of today's international pop stars. Music unites, integrates, and overcomes borders—but what lies behind it? How big a role did the Ricordi family play in this unique cultural achievement? How, in the end, is an opera—itself a complex interplay of music, poetry, stage design, theatrical and vocal interpretation, and economic prowess—created and played out in a cultural setting?

We hope our exhibition will provide new answers to these questions. We have asked experts to illuminate important aspects of the company's 200-year-old history in the following sections of this catalog. The manuscript scores, original stage and costume designs, photographs, and correspondence not only depict the history of Italian opera over a 200-year period: they also bear witness to the cultural importance of an entrepreneurial spirit that was enormously successful from both an economic and an artistic viewpoint.

Thomas Rabe/*Chief Financial Officer of Bertelsmann AG & President, Ricordi & C. SpA*

PRELUDE · Uwe R. Brückner

Io riscontro sempre più nel mio caro papà Giulio un sentimento grande di delicatezza e un affetto che (può star certo) è ricambiato a forti dosi. E la ringrazio per l'interesse che ha per me e che ha sempre avuto dal giorno che ebbi la fortuna d'incontrarlo.

I am ever more aware of a strong sense of discretion and affection in my dear papà Giulio that (you may be certain) is most warmly reciprocated. And I thank you for the interest you have and have always had in me from the day I was fortunate enough to meet you.

Giacomo Puccini to Giulio Ricordi/*Torre del Lago 11 October 1899*

In Western Europe, museums continue to receive far more visitors than all sports events combined. Increasingly, temporary exhibitions have become especially attractive formats for offering exceptional or even unconventional access to art collections or archives. Indeed, we are witnessing a boom of very successful thematic exhibitions, and not only at major museums like the Guggenheim Museum in Bilbao, Tate Modern in London, the Centre Pompidou in Paris, or the Neue Nationalgalerie in Berlin. Exhibitions have become a medium of "edutainment" as a way to present sophisticated historic, scientific, and popular themes to a diverse audience.

Does this format match the expectations of presenting a subject like opera, whose essence is in the directness of performance and the real-time experience? Is it possible to achieve a transformation of its dynamics into the more-or-less static format that exhibitions traditionally pretend to be? Yes, it is indeed.

Both formats—the theater and the exhibition—use the same resources by synchronizing them in a defined and choreographed space of light, sound, time-based media, and setting. Scenography means having an "orchestra" of media, which are ultimately composed and defined in a kind of score. These several media are comparable to musical instruments, each playing a major part in a specific area or time-frame. Together, they form a body composed of space, sound, narrative, and emotion.

Theater stages have their own rules; they are spaces with their own narrative relevance and usually offer the public a fixed viewpoint. In an exhibition, the visitors can stroll around; they constitute an anarchical and independent parameter, which must be taken into account. Opening opera to a wide audience means giving access to the backstage world both physically (in the scenography) and conceptually (in the storytelling).

The backstage world is structured in the dramaturgical order of the five stages incorporated in five installation cubes featuring "libretto," "score," "theatrical scenography," "voices and costumes," and finally "the representation"—the climax when all the elements come together in a performance. The five stages create a choreographed path that allows the visitor to understand the genesis of an opera—the "making of." The exhibition is like a window that offers an insightful view into the complex world of writing, composing, singing, conducting, or staging an opera and opens a door to all those workshops that are usually reserved "for staff only."

The scenography that frames the entire path generates a typical backstage atmosphere. The fully accessible environments create both an individual and a collective spatial experience. Watching artists paint a backdrop or tailors sew a costume, or strolling through an orchestra pit, are some of these three-dimensional adventures. We call it "staging the stage."

Paper begins to speak, the scores whisper melodies, and the word is given to the protagonists. In this kind of scenography, the visitors take part; they become actors in an installation, what Richard Wagner would call a *Gesamtkunstwerk*—a "total artwork"—according to his conception of the music drama. In the figurative sense this backstage environment literally plays with the metaphor of Ricordi's legendary engagement and carefully balanced relationship with all their divas, composers, and clients.

That's Opera – 200 Years of Italian Music provides an exciting access to one of the most fascinating collections of autographs, manuscript and rare printed librettos, letters, and original sketches of stage and costume designs, which was collected under the patronage of the Ricordis in their multiple function of music publishers, impresarios, artists, and close friends. The exhibition intends not only to satisfy experts, but also to attract a new audience and aims to reach those who never thought that opera would have interested them at all.

The unique scenography of the exhibit will create an emotional and lasting memory, a sort of corporate relationship between the fascinating world of opera and the visitors, just like the Ricordis achieved through their entrepreneurial spirit and unconditional passion for opera.

Uwe R. Brückner/*Creative Director, Atelier Brückner*

CONTENTS

THAT'S OPERA

Publisher as Protagonist:
Casa Ricordi

GABRIELE DOTTO

The three intertwined rings • Ricordi Logo since the 1870s
• Detail taken from the title page of the *Rivista minima* (1875)

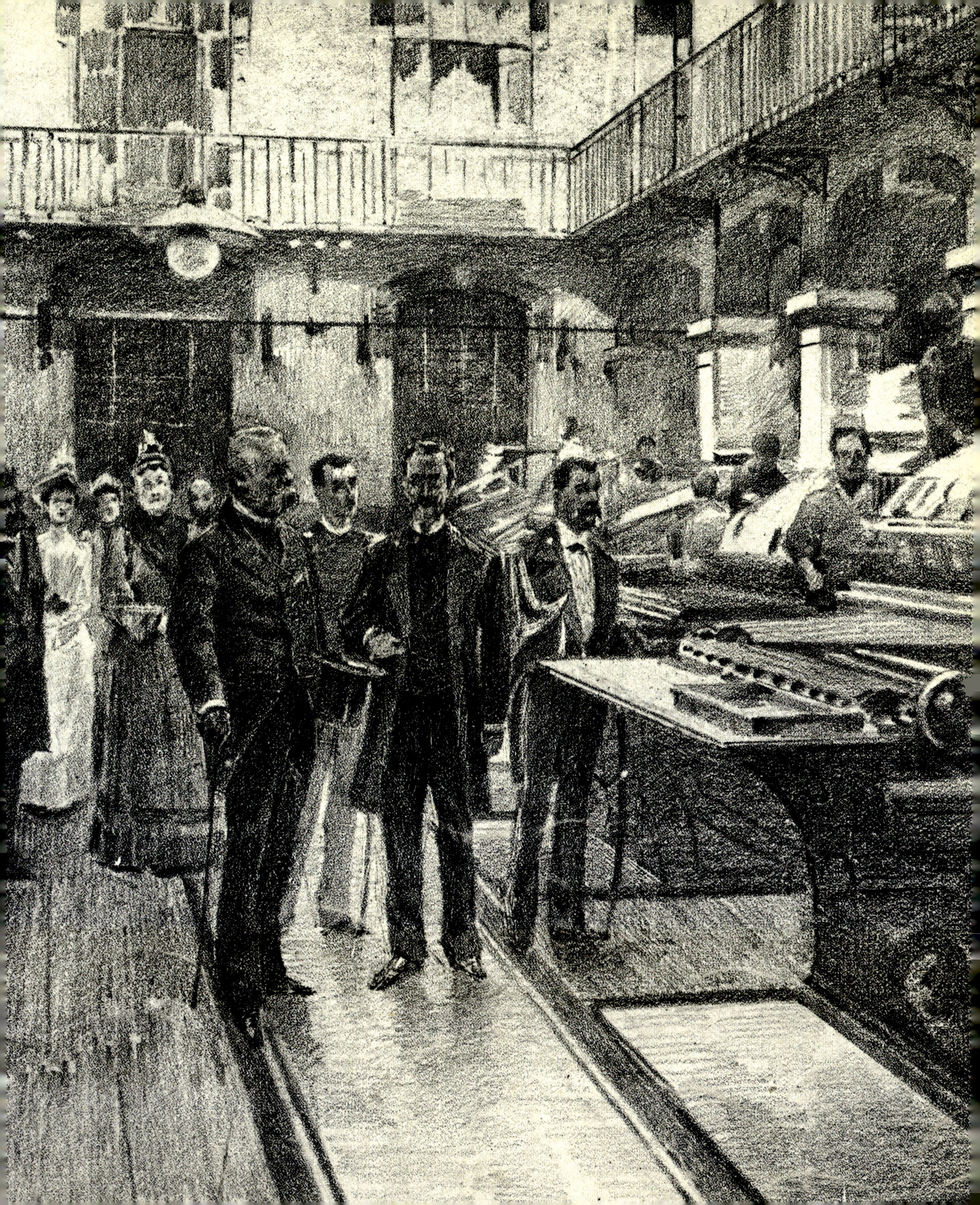

Publisher as Protagonist: Casa Ricordi

GABRIELE DOTTO

Quick: Who was the main publisher of Beethoven? Or of Mozart? Or of Brahms, Tchaikovsky, Chopin, or Debussy? A professional music historian may know the answers without having to consult an encyclopedia (though probably not), and a music aficionado may recall an occasional name.

In the case of Beethoven for instance, the publisher-composer Anton Diabelli might spring to mind, since Beethoven wrote a famous series of variations on one of his themes. But for the most part, those music publishers who were historically connected to major composers or specific music genres are hardly household names today, and even in their own time (though they were key players in the dissemination of the musical art, especially from the 19th century on) they rarely entered the limelight of popular perception.

Yet there is at least one striking exception to that pattern. Not only scholars of Italian music, but opera lovers in general, immediately recognize the name of Ricordi of Milan: as "the" publisher of Verdi; as "the" publisher of Puccini; as the principal (or the most memorable) publisher of Rossini, Donizetti, Bellini, and a host of others; as a name tied as closely to Italian opera of the so-called "Golden Century" (that is, from the early 19th century through the first quarter of the 20th) as those of the composers themselves. Indeed, many music buffs may more readily recognize the Ricordi name than they do those, for instance, of an opera's librettist or certainly of its first performers. How one music publisher should have achieved a sort of "star status" of name recognition almost on par with that of the most famous creators, interpreters, designers, and producers of opera is a story both fascinating and, in many ways, unique.

Of course, the history of Casa Ricordi is not about opera alone—indeed, its earliest printed editions were of instrumental chamber music—and with a catalog that has now reached, in this 200th year of the publisher's activity, the impressive threshold of 140,000 editions, it is clear that the Ricordi imprint has appeared on an enormous range of every conceivable type of music publication. Further, Ricordi also earned part of its worldwide fame in the late 19th and early 20th centuries through extra-musical items like the stunning graphic designs of the impressive team of artists working at its Arti Grafiche division (whose Art Nouveau posters are highly prized by collectors today). And in the late 20th century, "serious" music publishing at Ricordi became synonymous with cutting-edge *avant-garde* composers, many of whom purposefully avoided writing music for the stage in the 1950s, '60s and early '70s. But there is no ignoring the fact that Ricordi remains, in the mind of the broader public, a publisher first and foremost of opera, and from a commercial point of view, opera was the economic mainstay of the company's fortunes for the greater part of its history.

To begin at the beginning: Giovanni Ricordi, principal violinist at a small theater in Milan (a city full of theaters and above

Ricordi shop and offices in the building attached to the Teatro alla Scala • early 19th century • Lithograph by Alessandro Sanquirico

Antica sede della Casa editrice G. Ricordi & C. nell'edificio del Teatro alla Scala di Milano

Publisher as Protagonist: Casa Ricordi

GABRIELE DOTTO

all of the Teatro alla Scala, built in 1778 and host to an enormous number of important premières over the course of the next 150 years, ultimately coming to be considered the most prestigious venue for Italian opera in the world) who also played, conducted, or acted as prompter in several other small city theaters, began rounding out his income by offering his services as a music copyist. In this age of photo and digital reproduction we lose sight of the prodigious amount of hand-copying that went on during the 18th and 19th centuries, where all manner of documents had to be reproduced, in numbers too few to justify typesetting and printing, but cumulatively representing virtual mountains of copied paper. And at a time and place such as turn-of-the-century Milan at the dawning of the 1800s with its plethora of music venues, there was no paucity of work for a quick and able copyist; in short order, his income from these services outstripped that as a musician. In 1806, when he contracted with the Teatro Carcano to provide exclusive services as a copyist, he also worked out an agreement whereby he would become the owner of the parts he copied. It was a win-win scenario: the theater freed itself of a logistical bother (in an age in which the typical opera or ballet season featured as many or more new works as repeat productions, the sheer amount of paper accumulated—orchestra scores, vocal parts, instrumental parts, piano-rehearsal reductions—required expensive space and personnel to maintain) and Ricordi, above and beyond the one-off work of copying, began to build a library of musical materials he could rent to other theaters. Once copied, but many times used: the seed was planted for what would become his formal career as a publisher. A year later, in a contract with another Milanese theater (the Lentasio), Ricordi obtained the concession to sell publications derived from the operas and ballets he copied (extracts, reductions, and the like). It was time to explore the business of printed music. In the summer of 1807, Giovanni departed for what was then the world center for music publishing, Leipzig, for an intense apprenticeship in music engraving, printing, and production organization at the grand old firm of Breitkopf & Härtel (founded in 1719 and today the world's oldest active music publisher). By January of 1808, he was ready to establish his own publishing company.

Those beginnings set the stage for what could have been a perfectly decorous but potentially uneventful publishing career, and would not have necessarily foretold the meteoric success the newly founded publishing house would come to enjoy over the next few decades. In those early years of the 19th century, music publishing—indeed, even most book publishing—was only occasionally a significantly lucrative activity. In many cases, lovely editions of music were published due to the private passion and open sense of pride of the publisher, rather than from expectations of financial success. As Franz Liszt would write to Ricordi in 1838 (after a visit to Milan that left the composer-pianist filled with admiration for Ricordi's activity), referring to a set of virtuoso piano arrangements of Schubert songs he'd given Ricordi to publish: "I won't even mention those devilish melodies of Schubert of which, God knows, you won't even sell three copies!" But what distinguished the particular character of the Ricordi enterprise was that it represented something of a dichotomy: on the one hand, the methodical, lengthy preparation and printing of transcriptions, arrangements, or original pieces of sheet music—an elegant and quiet activity; on the other hand, the madcap rush to prepare, revise, and rapidly supply huge amounts of musical material in the frenzied world of 19th-century opera production, where entire operas might be written, rehearsed, and performed in a matter of weeks, requiring a large staff of collaborators and superlative organizational skills. As opposed to the genteel and calm activity of preparing and selling printed music, the involvement with theaters staging newly composed works was (and can still be) highly participatory and dynamic. For this second type of activity Giovanni Ricordi's unique background in the theater as both performer and copyist provided excellent experience, and his keen sense of economy and talent for logistics, as well as a sharp commercial acumen, provided a stabilizing element in a highly volatile business environment. The risks could be enormous, but so could the rewards.

Some luck, of course, was also involved. No matter how creative and energetic an entrepreneur Giovanni was, had it not been for the concomitant exponential rise of opera as popular entertainment (and the rise of a bourgeois class with more elevated cultural aspirations) he might not have been as successful as he was. There is little doubt he was quite good at what he did—indeed, brilliant—since there were literally hundreds of publishers old and new scattered throughout Europe, but few had as impressively quick or resounding a success as he did. Yet perhaps not even Giovanni, when he started the business, could have imagined the speed and extent of his firm's expansion. Had he begun his publishing activity thirty years earlier, for instance, he might not have found the occasion for such rapid success. Instead, it was a propitious moment for him to dive headlong into the business of acquiring the rights to operas and to manage the supply of material, thanks to a confluence of fortuitous events: the musical and theatrical life of Milan, which had already been quite lively under the dominion of

Giovanni Ricordi • circa 1850 • Lithograph by Antonio Bignoli

Publisher as Protagonist: Casa Ricordi

GABRIELE DOTTO

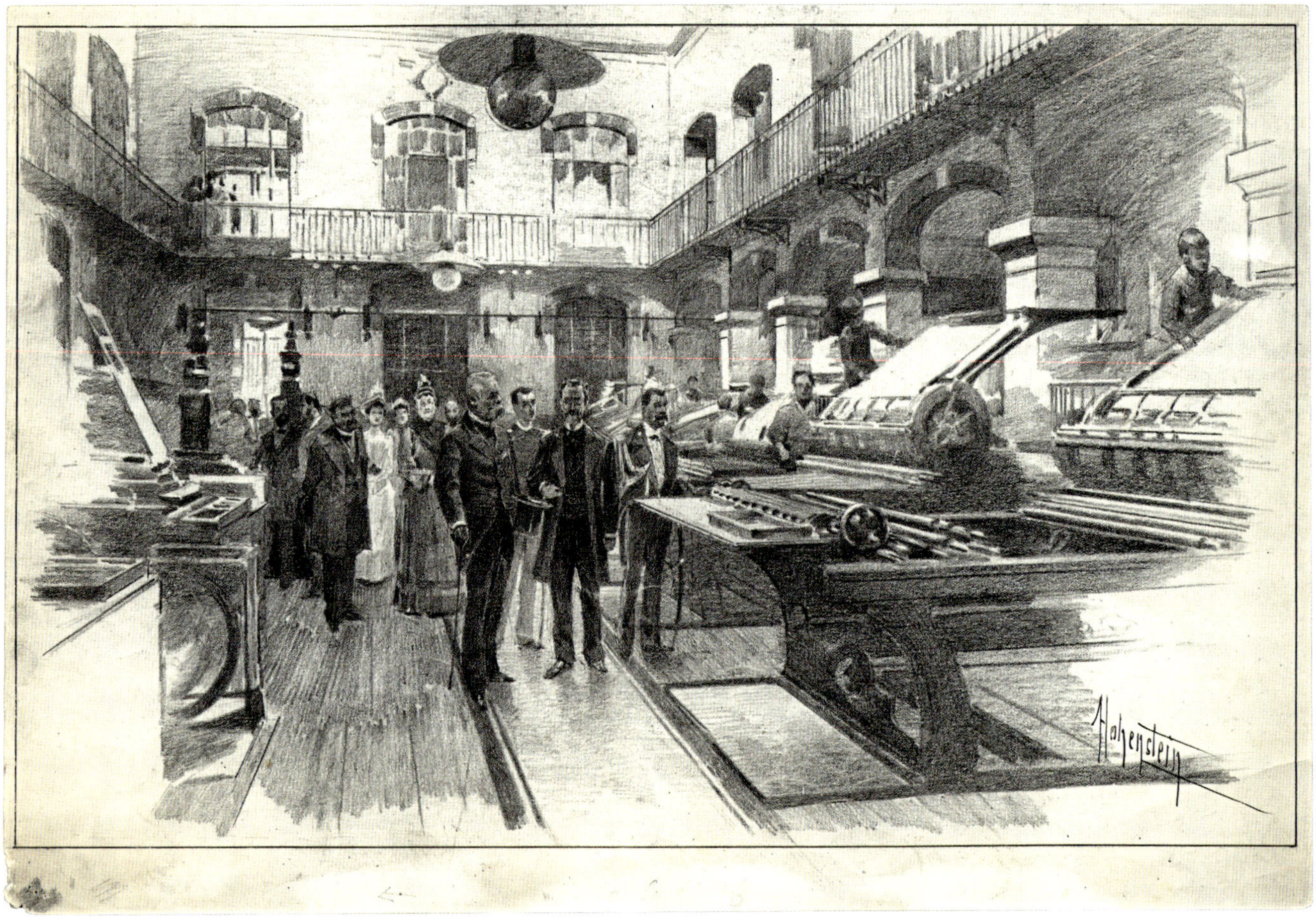

Maria Theresa and the Austrian empire, became significantly more active after the arrival of Napoleon, with the blossoming of a prodigious amount of publishing activity, diminished censorship, the opening of public entertainment to a broader audience, the founding of a music conservatory, and so forth. At the same time, the groundswell of popularity of Italian opera throughout Europe that had begun in the late 1700s began to intensify in the new century, and its newest young star, Gioachino Rossini, rode the wave brilliantly to become perhaps the most celebrated composer in Europe by the time of his early retirement around 1830. As mentioned, the roots of opera's popularity were also nourished by the intense desire of the growing bourgeoisie and the entrepreneurial *nouveau riche* of the industrial revolution to enjoy the cultural offerings that had previously been the almost exclusive domain of the aristocracy. Further, by mid-century the expanding European railroad network made it possible for Italian singers and opera companies to travel rapidly from city to city and for a publisher like Ricordi to quickly supply the materials necessary for performance. Hence Casa Ricordi was perfectly positioned to draw the greatest benefit from this enormously expanding interest in Italian opera.

This is an appropriate point to recall why opera (which was invented in Italy around 1600 as an ideal wedding of vocal and instrumental expression and dramatic spectacle) had come to be such an overwhelming presence in Italian music-making in the 19th century, to the near exclusion of most other musical forms. While in the rest of Europe, instrumental music (for large or small groups), chamber vocal music, and choral music enjoyed (proportionally) far greater success than in Italy, there was no dearth of opera composing in northern Europe, and indeed

King Umberto I visits the Ricordi printing plant
• Drawing by Adolf Hohenstein, 1890

some of the greatest and most innovative "Italian" style operas were written by composers like Handel, Gluck, and of course Mozart. Conversely, there was no dearth in Italy of excellent composers of music for solo instruments, for chorus, or for instrumental ensemble (in fact, historians credit the Milanese composer Giovanni Sammartini with the development of the symphony, which would flourish instead in Northern Europe). But opera in Italy came to overshadow other musical forms because the human voice continued to be considered the ideal and most noble musical instrument, and the Italian love of spectacle was insatiable; thus opera came to be considered the highest expression of a "total" representative artwork.

Back to Casa Ricordi. The company's growth was astonishing, fed both by its vertiginous acquisition of new works and by the absorption of theatrical archives and of other publishing firms. By 1813 Ricordi was the owner of 800 scores; by 1825 the firm's first published *Grande catalogo* offered 2,247 printed editions and over 1,000 operas available for hire. A mere quarter century after its founding, Ricordi was the largest music publisher in southern Europe. In 1838 the number of hire scores listed in its catalog had risen to 1,800 and the number of printed editions to 10,000. The imposing catalog of 1844—described by the historian Claudio Sartori as a "milestone" in the company's history—definitively established Casa Ricordi's domination of the field. An article in a Milanese trade publication of 1845 (*Lo spettatore industriale*) observed: "The catalog of music published by signor Ricordi includes more than *seventeen thousand* editions, a staggering number, especially when one considers that the most famous publishers of France and Germany, many of whom began operations even thirty years before Ricordi, barely reach 8,000 editions."

(That same *Spettatore industriale* article offers insight into the precious collection that would become today's Historical Archive: "We cannot omit mention of the great archive of original manuscripts comprising over two thousand opera scores, several hundred of which are autographs. For the *aficionado* lovers of music—especially when they are British, it seems—the supreme goal of a visit to the Ricordi offices is the chance to see the original autographs of, for instance, Rossini's *Gazza ladra* and *L'italiana in Algeri*, of Bellini's *Sonnambula* and *Straniera*, of Donizetti's *Anna Bolena* and *Lucrezia Borgia*, Mercadante's *Giuramento*, etc. etc." Somewhat unexpectedly, we learn from this article that, already more than a century and a half ago, the Ricordi archive was already famous. What had begun as a commercial expedient—the careful preservation of original documents in order to ensure exploitation rights and guard against all manner of piracy, in an era before clear-cut laws on intellectual property had been established throughout Italy and Europe—became a private "collector's" passion of each generation to follow.)

Naturally success breeds success, and as the firm grew it became a magnet for the finest Italian opera composers of the day. Giovanni also soon developed an uncanny sense for choosing the most promising young composers, a talent that subsequently manifested itself in the entire Ricordi dynasty. When the twenty-year-old Rossini received his first commission for an opera in Milan, Ricordi immediately secured the rights while other publishers were watching and waiting. That opera—*La pietra del paragone*—was a huge success and the definitive launch of the young composer's career. The collaboration and warm friendship with Rossini would continue thereafter. Donizetti would consider Ricordi his main publisher and Bellini, at first cautious, eventually came round to regarding Ricordi as a trusted ally and in 1834 proposed an exclusive contract. In 1839, Ricordi lost no time in acquiring the rights to Verdi's first opera and went on to publish nearly all of his works. And to remain just with the five foremost figures of Italian opera's Golden Century—though of course Ricordi acquired the works of many other fine composers of opera in that same period—Giovanni's grandson Giulio published Puccini's first opera and famously stood by the young composer even when, following the failure of both that and his next opera, the Ricordi board of directors complained that the youngster failed to show promise. Time, of course, proved Giulio's intuition to be correct, and Puccini became an astonishing success.

Innovative and efficient production techniques, a wide distribution network, and a special gift for divining talent, however, are not in themselves sufficient to guarantee success. Publishing is also very much about relationships and an interactive endeavor, and in the complex world of music in the theater at the level in which the Ricordi firm became involved—as project coordinators, even (eventually) as impresarios themselves—it meant commissioning and organizing the work of teams of skilled artists and balancing and mitigating the enormous stresses inevitably generated when the creative pace clashed with inescapable deadlines. When we appreciate the result of these creative forces we lose sight of the fact that the genesis of all these works involved logistical nightmares, battles with theater managements, conflicts with censors, authorial procrastination, and all manner of last-minute production disaster. And as much as we admire these great artists, we also tend to overlook the presence of many massive egos, often irascible, all too often petty.

Publisher as Protagonist: Casa Ricordi

GABRIELE DOTTO

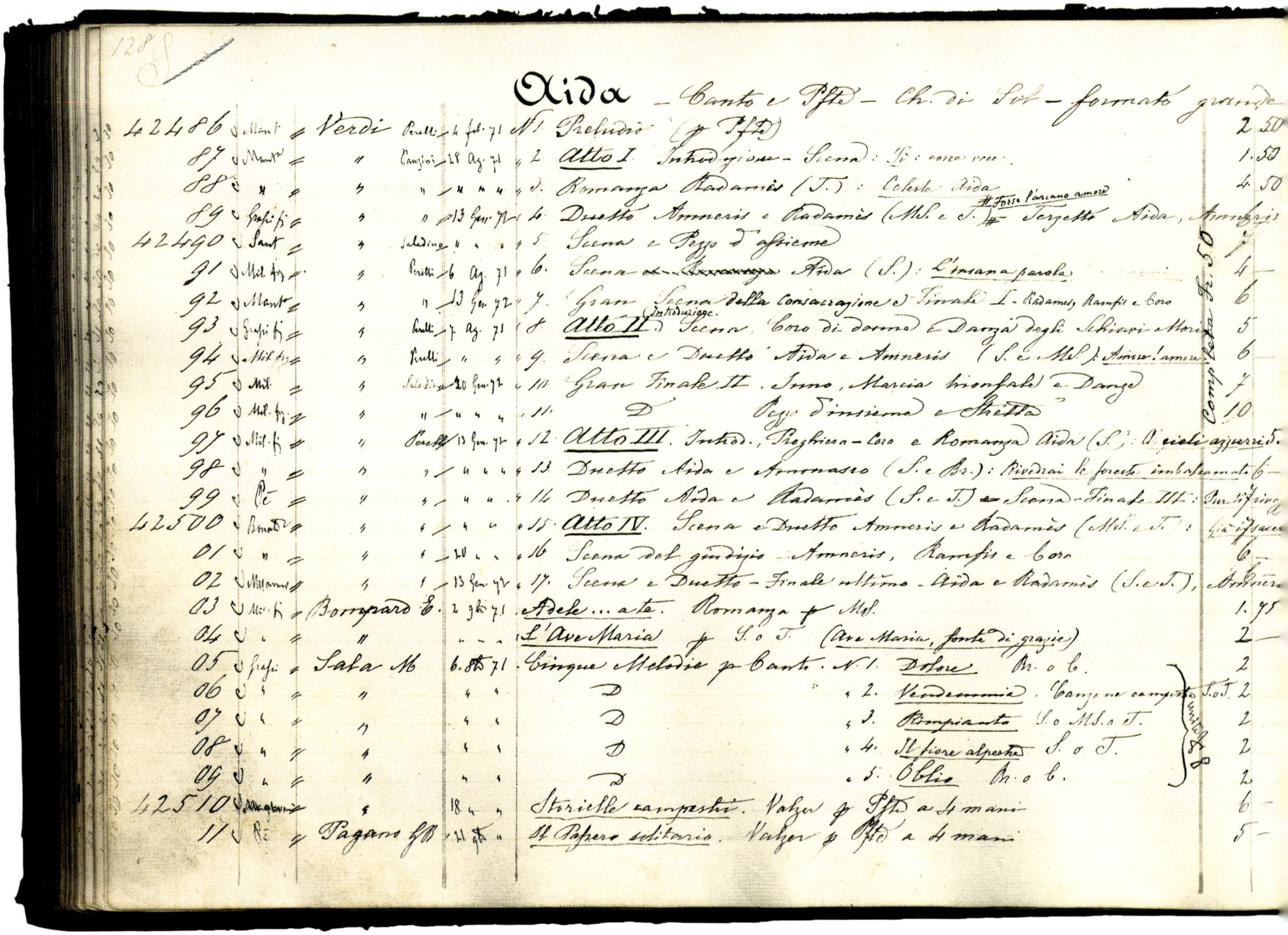

Original Casa Ricordi production ledger (one of the so-called "libroni")
• The editors logged new works to be assigned to the copyists (for hire material) or to the engravers (for hire or printed editions)

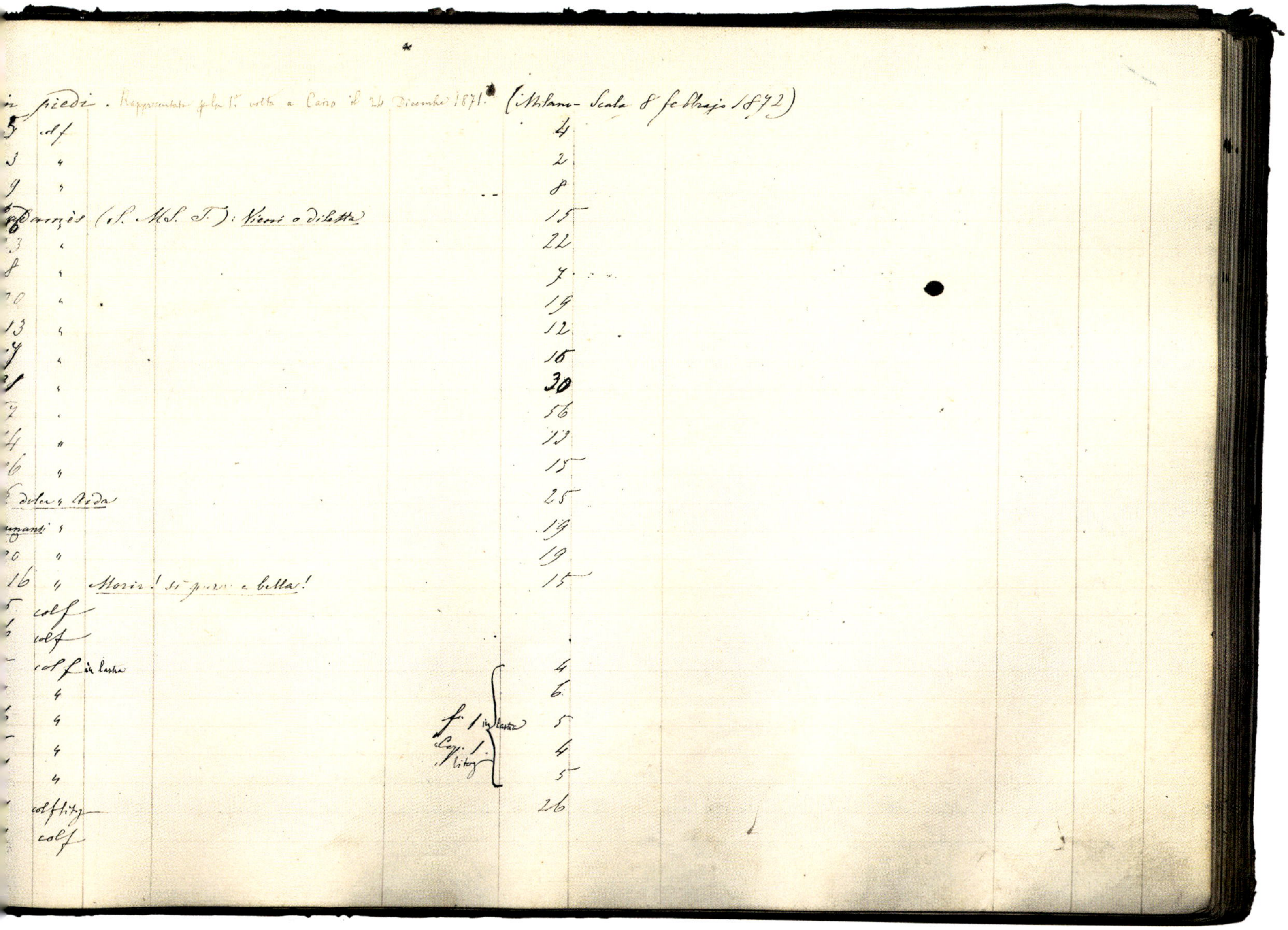
piedi. Rappresentata per la 1a volta a Cairo il 24 Dicembre 1871. (Milano – Scala 8 febbrajo 1872)

5 colf 4
3 " 2
9 " 8
Parigi (S. MS. T.): Vieni o diletta 15
3 " 22
8 " 7
10 " 19
13 " 12
7 " 16
1 " 30
2 " 56
4 "
6 " 15
dolce Aida 25
" 19
10 " 19
16 " Morir! sì pura e bella! 15
colf
colf
colf in lastra 4
" 6
" f. 1 in lastra 5
" Cop. 1 4
" litog. 5
colf litog 26
colf

Publisher as Protagonist:
Casa Ricordi

GABRIELE DOTTO

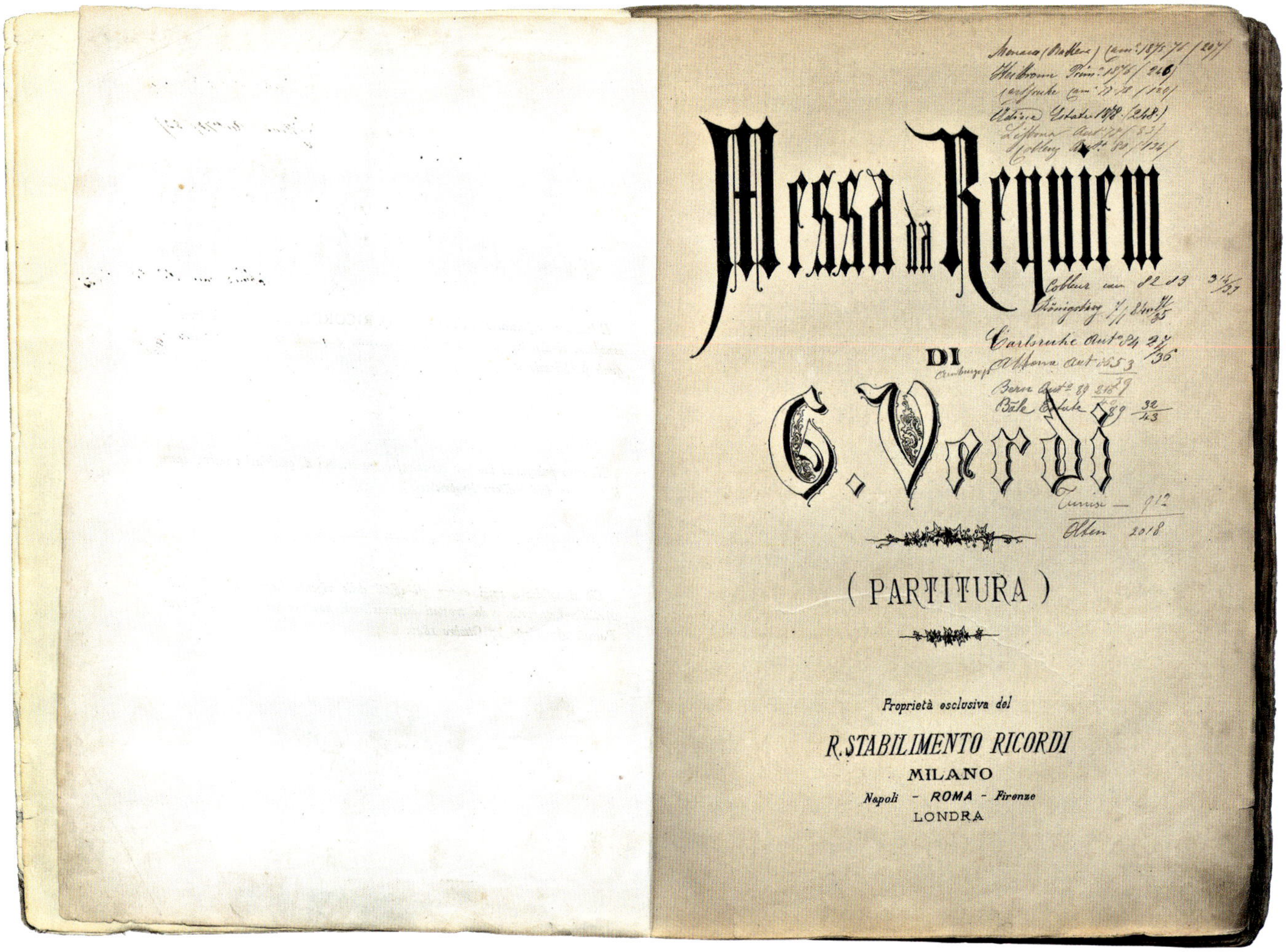

Being a publisher meant being at one and the same time advisor, psychologist, diplomat, and, of course, trusted friend. Verdi, as is well known, saw in Giovanni a reliable mentor and Puccini looked to Giulio almost as father figure. Further, the fact that operas are a *collaborative* art form (notwithstanding our curious practice of identifying an opera by the composer's name alone) meant that in moments of crisis the publisher often had to act as mediator among opposing forces. The collaboration between the librettist team of Luigi Illica-Giuseppe Giacosa and Giacomo Puccini—for *La bohème*, *Tosca*, and *Madama Butterfly*—is abundantly emblematic. Many were the times Giulio had to intervene directly to soothe bruised feelings, find mutually agreeable compromises, spur the work onward, or neutralize threats from one or another party to abandon the work altogether. Giacosa wrote this to Giulio on 6 October 1893, while working on *Bohème*:

> Dear Ricordi,
> I quit. I'll send you that little bit that I think is presentable, out of the considerable amount of work I've done. [...] I can work at writing that requires thought and careful reasoning but not in a train-of-thought way ... If Puccini weren't in a rush, if he could concentrate on setting to music the third act which I sent him practically in final form and give me more time to work on this second act perhaps my inspiration would return [...] I respect you too much to want to put you in an embarrassing position and thus I take this heroic

Messa da Requiem, Giuseppe Verdi
• The first edition full score used for the hire library

> choice of pulling out of the enterprise, as I am sure that Illica can perfectly well finish it on his own [...] But I ask you one thing, which is: even though I realize my decision is extremely damaging for you, I hope you will not be angry with me. I consider as a very precious thing to have you as a fine and constant friend.

Illica to Giulio, end of October:

> The other day [...] I learned—and this doesn't surprise me—that Puccini has barely worked at all [on *Bohème*]. But between working slowly, and changing your mind and wanting to work on something else, there is a huge difference. [...] I know full well that Puccini is like a clock that starts and stops easily. [...] But in the *Bohème* project [should it fail] we all stand to lose face. [...] So please, don't let Puccini have his way in this.
>
> He has to finish *Bohème*, finish it quickly, and well, so that he can reach that success that you and I both know he can obtain.

Puccini to Giulio (who had called a meeting between the composer and Illica), the following 21 July:

> I'll come to your office Tuesday at 10 as you ask.
>
> I find Illica's irritation odd and it surprises me. When he came here we were in perfect agreement [...] and deplored that I was not going forward with *Bohème* and said he would agree with everything I asked. Now that I have seen him again he enjoys putting on airs, and if he says I've set the work aside, whose fault is it? The work needed only be what it should be, that is, logical, tightly written, interesting, and balanced. But up until now, it's been nothing of the sort. Must I accept Illica's gospel with my eyes shut?

Giulio to Illica, 24 July:

> Puccini is here. I had written you asking you to join us this morning at 10. Did you not get the letter? Look, whether you prefer a wrestling bout or a boxing match, this situation has to end once and for all!!!

La bohème, of course, was finally completed and became the worldwide success we all know. But for Giulio—on this, as on many other projects—its preparation must have seemed like pulling teeth.

Publishers, patrons, and impresarios, mediators and formidable negotiators, the four generations of the Ricordi dynasty also proved to be indefatigable entrepreneurs. Under Tito I the production offices expanded and the firm began producing graphic artwork; the first branch offices opened in Italy and later in other countries; other publishing houses were absorbed, including Ricordi's most tenacious rival in the field of opera, Casa Lucca; and he carried forward the push (initiated by Giovanni) toward full recognition of intellectual property rights of music. Giulio expanded the network of affiliate offices and placed particular emphasis on the journalistic arm of the company, relaunching the influential *Gazzetta musicale*, later *Musica e musicisti* and ultimately *Ars et labor*. The 1902 *Nuovo Gran Catalogo* of Ricordi publications reached the milestone of 100,000 titles.

On 7 June 1912 the news of Giulio's death received a full column in the *New York Times* with the headline "Giulio T. Ricordi dies in Milan / Head of the Famous Music Publishing House [that] controlled the Works of Verdi, Puccini and Others." The article went on to state: "The firm has been called 'The Operatic Trust' because it has such a secure hold upon the music publishing business of the world." Heady words. If viewed from the vantage point of the America of Theodore Roosevelt and W.H. Taft who crusaded to break up the "trusts" of Big Oil, Big Steel, and the like, Casa Ricordi became typecast as Big Music. (And no doubt, many a miserly opera administrator must have resented the imposing presence of a powerful publisher intent on ensuring that its stable of authors received their—and its—full fair share of royalty income from lucrative performances that made the fortune of opera managers around the world.) Surely the thought that the company founded by a humble music copyist of Milan, who barely more than a century before could be found curved over his open-air copydesk near *Piazza dei mercanti* briskly turning out handwritten sheets of music, should be defined by the leading newspaper of one of the world's financial capitals as the powerhouse of the music publishing world, would have prompted a wry smile on Giovanni Ricordi's face.

Giulio was a very hard act to follow. The last of the direct line of Ricordis to serve as chief administrator of the firm, Tito II inherited the arduous task of directing a publishing concern in times of general economic instability and, ultimately, through the crisis of World War I. No one could foresee it at the time, of course, but the flush years of the enormous popularity of new Italian opera were also about to run their course. Significantly, it was Puccini's last opera—the unfinished *Turandot*, performed posthumously in 1926, after Tito II had left the firm—that would,

Publisher as Protagonist:
Casa Ricordi

GABRIELE DOTTO

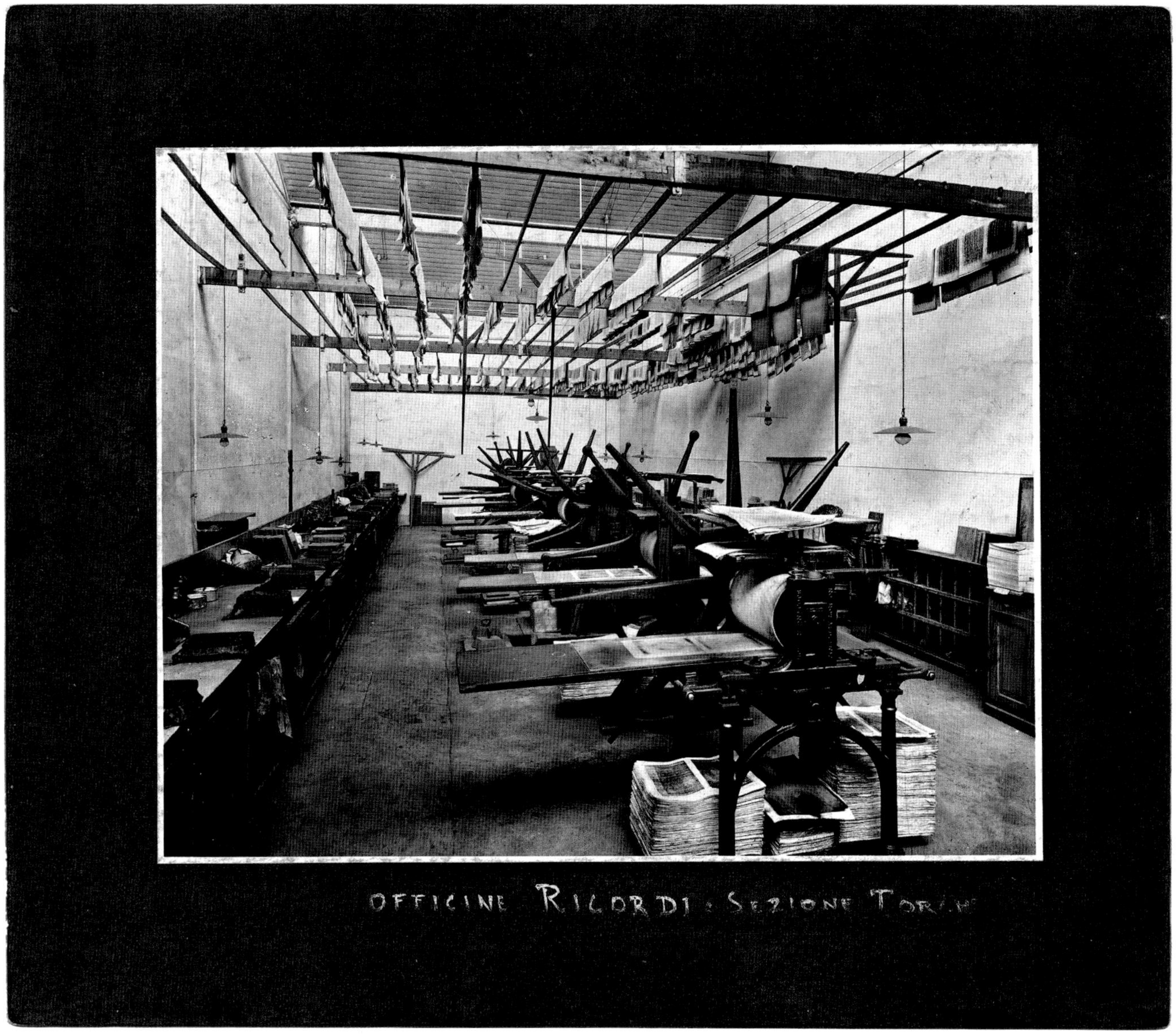

Printing machines in the Viale Campania plant, Milan
• early 20th century

Ricordi shop in London
• early 20th century

ARS ET LABOR
MAINTIENDRAI
FERT FERT
63
265 G. RICORDI & Co. 265
AND AT
MILAN, ROME, NAPLES
PALERMO AND PARIS.
RICORDI
AND AT
MILAN, ROME, NAPLES,
PALERMO AND PARIS.
RICORDI
RAILWA
ST PROP
BRELLAS
LADIES' TAILOR
Hyman
FURRIER
RAILWAY
LOST
PROPERTY
2/
UMBRELLAS
UP-STAIRS
GOOD-BYE
PARTED
F. PAOLO TOSTI
MANON LESCAUT
AIDA
RICORDI
RICORDI

Publisher as Protagonist:
Casa Ricordi

GABRIELE DOTTO

in hindsight, mark the end of what has come to be defined as the Golden Century of Italian opera—an impressive string of masterworks starting with Rossini's *Barbiere* that have remained in the repertory to this day.

To be sure, while Casa Ricordi continued to expand its catalog of symphonic, choral, and chamber music, it also continued acquiring and commissioning new operas throughout the 1930s and '40s, including excellent works by such authors as Alfano, Malipiero, Montemezzi, Pizzetti, Zandonai, and many others. But opera houses and opera audiences—in no small way influenced by the rapid emergence of recorded music—were increasingly interested in hearing the canon of established favorites and, in a reversal of what had been the norm a century before, the performance of new operas became a small minority of opera programming. Opera performance continued to have a dedicated public, but by the post-World War II era the programming focused almost exclusively on repertory works.

Modern times. The arrival of the *avant-garde* movements of the 1950s and '60s revealed, in some quarters, something of a love-hate relationship of modern composers with opera. Perhaps as a reaction to the overwhelming dominance of the operatic form in Italy, there seemed to be in those years, among the new generation of the time, much more interest in opera among Northern European composers than in the land of opera's birth; a few Italian *avant-garde* composers of the 1960s embraced the form and indeed wrote some striking works in the genre, but quite a few modernists of the late postwar era turned their attention to other genres. Casa Ricordi continued to champion the work of Italian opera composers, many of whom wrote in a more traditional compositional style, but the number of new operas produced in any given year was no longer large. Then, as the 1970s drew to a close, a new ferment of attraction toward the glorious old genre of opera—transformed, at times, to take on a much more variegated form than just that of a linear narrative set to music—seemed to take hold, both among the established generation of modernist composers and especially among the rising young generation born after the war. The 1980s saw a veritable boom of new operas from Italian composers (and increasing interest among non-Italian composers as well) in an array of musical styles, coinciding with the regenerated interest worldwide in traditional opera. A new (and gratifyingly younger) audience fell under the spell of opera in ever increasing numbers. Broadcast opera found audiences in the millions, and commissions for new operas began to enjoy a dramatic upswing. The ledgers of the Ricordi offices were once again filled with the production schedules of new works for the stage. In a poetic touch, as the 20th century drew to a close, one of the great Italian composers of the second half of that century, Luciano Berio, would conclude his own career of works for the stage with a completion of Puccini's unfinished *Turandot*.

Meantime, the traditional repertory of Italian opera also encountered something of a transformation. Thanks to the impassioned and patient work of music scholars, forgotten jewels of the past have been brought into the limelight, and even well-known works have been carefully stripped of layers of changes accumulated over time and restored to their original splendor, through the initiatives of the critical editions. Fittingly, the first important such initiative forty years ago was an edition of Rossini's *Barbiere di Siviglia*—the opera that, as mentioned above, historians mark as the beginning of Italian opera's Golden Century. In the intervening years, monumental editions of the works of Rossini, Verdi, and Donizetti, prepared in collaboration with or initiated by Casa Ricordi, have made a significant contribution to the revival of many beautiful works (or differing versions of well-known operas), to informing performance style, and to our understanding of opera history. The recently launched editions of the works of Bellini and Puccini promise to do the same.

A renewed audience, a renewed traditional repertory, and a renewed interest in new operas. At the dawn of Ricordi's third century, its connection to the repertory with which it is most identified is indeed undergoing an impressive rebirth. And the grand old house of Ricordi—not only a "printer and supplier of music" but at times also advisor, organizer, and even impresario—finds itself still occupying a central role of publisher and protagonist.

Constructing an Opera:
The Ideas Behind an Exhibition

JEAN-JACQUES NATTIEZ

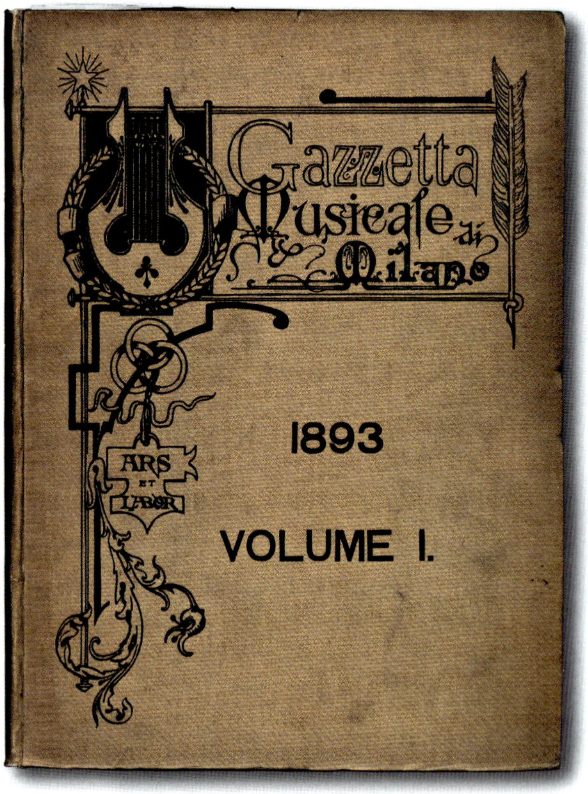

Gazzetta musicale di Milano • n.1, 1893
• Music journal founded by Giovanni and Tito I Ricordi in 1842

Giacomo Puccini, nicknamed "the Doge" • circa 1895
• With a dedication to Giulio Ricordi

il Doge

Constructing an Opera:
The Ideas Behind an Exhibition

JEAN-JACQUES NATTIEZ

For the majority of music and opera lovers, an opera is essentially a sung theatrical spectacle with stars and divas of both genders whose performances and recordings are ceaselessly compared and whose slightest shortcomings are dissected (opera audiences have long memories). The show is directed by a conductor who may be practically invisible, but it is he who is thought solely responsible for deciding on the tempos and dynamics of the musical interpretation.

People also know that what is seen on stage is the result of the diktats of an unseen director and of the aesthetic choices of the set and the costume designers: It is they who are chiefly responsible for the spectacle. In the Western world, opera is also a social ritual: opera buffs all dream of sitting at least once in their life in La Scala or Covent Garden, the Opéra-Bastille in Paris or the Metropolitan Opera House in New York, and attending the festivals at Bayreuth or Salzburg—even if buying tickets means enduring what amounts to an assault course.

Split into three distinct sections, the purpose of the present exhibit is to show that opera can be something more. First of all, the exhibition wants to underscore the key role played by a publisher in the genesis and dissemination of many operas: Casa Ricordi, the great Milanese music house. Secondly, it has chosen seven works so as to illustrate the progress of constructing an opera from the initial conception of the libretto and score to its stage production. Finally, the exhibition treats in a similar way two modern operas that are not very widely known, but which offer an opportune reminder that it is a living art and cannot be identified solely with the art of 19th-century *bel canto* or *verismo*.

Why has a special part of the exhibition been set aside for an account of the history of the Casa Ricordi? Primarily of course because the occasion celebrates the bicentenary of its establishment in 1808 by Giovanni Ricordi, who perfected a new system of distributing what is termed an opera's "performance material." If one is able to buy a full orchestral score or a reduction for voice and piano, individual orchestral and choral parts are, on the other hand, not sold but hired out. This eminently profitable system—a veritable publishing revolution that guaranteed income from the hire of the score, so allowing composers to free themselves from impresarios—made it possible for Ricordi to earn its place as one of the most successful music publishers, including in its catalog the "big five" of 19th- and early 20th-century opera: Rossini, Bellini, Donizetti, Verdi, and Puccini. Through a wealth of photographs as well as important letters, the exhibition demonstrates how the four members of the Ricordi dynasty, Giovanni, Tito I, Giulio, and Tito II, were not only publishers, but men capable of helping their artists bring their projects to completion. Thanks to this hire system—later adopted by almost all publishers of symphonic music and opera around the world—the Ricordi house expanded, establishing itself in many major cities (Rome, London, São Paolo, New York, Buenos Aires, Paris, Toronto, etc.), and also, as early as 1808, acquiring and regularly upgrading some extremely sophisticated technical equipment. In 1871, even a "school for

Prometeo, Luigi Nono • Venice, Chiesa di San Lorenzo, 1984
• Autograph score

30
4 Vni
Vle + VC + CB
ASCOLTA,
MAESTRO DEL GIOCO
CORO
S.
A.
T.
B.
FL.B.
Frullato aria intonata
LOCO
ARIA INTONATA
ARIA FRULLATA
CLKB
CON BOCCHINO
TUBA LOCO
GLAS
Heiner
Barbara
Vle
VC
CB

Constructing an Opera:
The Ideas Behind an Exhibition

JEAN-JACQUES NATTIEZ

music engraving" was created. By the end of the 19th century, Casa Ricordi was printing some 25 million sheets of music a year. Ricordi also acquired the distribution and production rights for works published outside Italy, as well as buying up smaller publishers such as Casa Lucca which represented Wagner in Italy. A small area in the present exhibition illustrates the essential role Ricordi played in gaining acceptance for the German composer in the peninsula, Wagner being an example of what Ricordi did for many other non-Italian composers. The company also benefited from a fine sense for marketing, bringing out magazines such as the *Gazzetta musicale di Milano* (launched in 1842) and *Musica e musicisti*, and printing posters, postcards, and other merchandise, eventually setting up the Atelier delle Officine Grafiche Ricordi in 1896. Ricordi also expanded into musical domains such as Lombard and Neapolitan song, light music (Tenco, Battisti, etc.), operetta (such as *Il tappeto rosa* by Jules Burgmein—the pseudonym of Giulio Ricordi, himself a composer), film music (that of Nino Rota, for example), and now publishes composers of music of the 20th and even 21st centuries (so Boito's *Nerone* has been followed by Luigi Nono's *Prometeo*, and works by Salvatore Sciarrino, Luciano Berio, and Fabio Vacchi). Casa Ricordi also publishes textbooks and teaching manuals such as the *Enciclopedia della musica* that appeared in 1964 and critical editions conforming to modern musicological principles of Italian composers such as Vivaldi, as well as of operas from its catalog, including those of Rossini, as well as scholarly studies of their original productions.

Collecting the documents for this exhibition has only been possible thanks to the fact that Casa Ricordi has collected the most important documents and material since its creation and had acquired other music archives, for instance those of La Scala in 1825. These archives astonish visitors with their enormous holdings, their accurate and painstaking cataloging, and an accessibility policy that should be the envy of many a public institution.

The bulk of the exhibit is devoted to the successive phases in the conception and realization of an opera distributed into five "cubes" which aim to present and describe them:

The Libretto *(Libretto. Find the right words.)*
The Score *(Partitura. Tell it through the notes.)*
The Production *(Scenografia. Put it on stage.)*
Voices and costumes *(Voci e costumi. Feel the emotions.)*
The Performance *(Rappresentazione. Enjoy the show.)*

Each of the five cubes devoted to these phases going from the literary and musical idea for an opera to its performance on stage is illustrated by seven Italian operas that serve as a thread running through the whole exhibition and that reappear from cube to cube:

Giuseppe Verdi (1813–1900):
Aida (1871)
Falstaff (1893)

Puccini (1858–1924):
La bohème (1896)
Tosca (1900)
Madama Butterfly (1904)

And a pair of modern operas:
Prometeo (1984–85) by Luigi Nono (1924–90)
Teneke (2007) by Fabio Vacchi (born 1947).

Each of the seven operas is present in one way or another in each of the five cubes, though the emphasis is placed each time on just one. The libretto section focuses on *La bohème*; the score on the original manuscripts of *Aida* and *Teneke*; production on *Tosca*; voices and costumes on *Madama Butterfly*; and for performance once again on *Aida*.

Today the words "exhibit designer" designate the person, in this case Uwe Brückner, responsible for "staging" the objects and documents presented in an exhibition. The situation here is rather unusual in that it is the opera itself that is staged, with the visitor participating in its gestation.

In the first cube (*Libretto*) that highlights *La bohème*, the visitor is invited, as in acts one and four of the opera, into a student's room. Visitors first head backstage, as it were, before entering a space in which they are able to hear various instruments from the score. For the third (*Scenografia*), they arrive in a painter's studio. For the fourth (*Costumi*), centered on *Madama Butterfly*, they enter a Japanese house with paper walls. For the fifth, they are invited into a theater. Let's retrace the route.

In the first cube, devoted mainly to the libretto of *La bohème*, visitors see first a photograph from 1896 showing Puccini and the opera's two librettists, Giuseppe Giacosa and Luigi Illica. An edition of the Henri Murger's novel reminds us that the opera was inspired by his *Scènes de la vie de bohème*. A few pages from the manuscript of the libretto in which Puccini's handwriting can be recognized show how the composer intervened in the work of his two collaborators. The presentation of certain

In the park of Giuseppe Verdi's villa in Sant'Agata • after 1897 →
• Seated, left to right: Maria Carrara Verdi, Barberina Strepponi, Giuseppe Verdi, and Giuditta Ricordi. Standing, left to right: Teresa Stolz, Umberto Campanari, Giulio Ricordi, and Leopoldo Metlicovitz

MILANO
Giulio Rossi
Carrara - Stolz
Strepponi
Barbara
Campanari
Verdi
Giulio Ricordi
Giuditta Ricordi

Constructing an Opera: The Ideas Behind an Exhibition

JEAN-JACQUES NATTIEZ

Giacomo Puccini (second from the right) flanked by Tito II and Puccini's son Antonio on board of the steamboat "George Washington" • on their way to the première of *La fanciulla del West* in New York, November 1910

musical sketches shows that the composition of the music for the opera did not necessarily begin once the libretto had been completed, but rather that the two progressed in tandem.

The second cube, dedicated to the score, provides a golden opportunity to show the exceptional richness of the Ricordi archives. First in view come facsimiles of scores of Paganini's *Capricci* (since Ricordi also published a great deal of instrumental music), of *La gazza ladra* by Rossini, *La sonnambula* by Bellini, *Don Pasquale* by Donizetti, *Otello* and *Falstaff* by Verdi, and Puccini's *Tosca*, as well as a few astonishing sheets from Nono's *Prometeo*. Then visitors enter what is a genuine "Aladdin's cave" where they are invited in total silence to admire the autograph score of *Aida* and some pages from Fabio Vacchi's *Teneke*, as well as from Boito's *Mefistofele*, Zandonai's *Francesca da Rimini*, and two operettas written under a pseudonym (Jules Burgmein) by Giulio Ricordi, *Il tappeto rosa* and *La secchia rapita*. But the experience does not stop there: in a third section, visitors listen to music from *Aida* (the triumphal march), *Falstaff* (the fugato), *La bohème* (the death of Mimi), *Tosca* (the death of Scarpia), and *Madama Butterfly* (the first-act duet) while virtually "flicking" through pages of the corresponding scores delivered electronically and interactively.

The third cube is devoted to staging and production—*Scenografia*. Mainly for *Tosca*, but also for *La bohème*, *Madama Butterfly*, *Aida*, and *Falstaff*, photographs dating from the premières of these operas present the real landscapes or monuments incorporated into the original sets dreamt up by Attilio Comelli, Adolf Hohenstein, Girolamo Magnani, Angelo Parravicini, and Vittorio Rota, as well as some admirable original designs in oils. As a contrast to the style of 19th- and early 20th-century stage design, the props and spaces conceived by the architect Renzo Piano for Luigi Nono's *Prometeo*, as well as sketches and sets by the sculptor Arnoldo Pomodoro for Fabbio Vacchi's *Teneke*, testify to the close links in our own time between cutting-edge visual art and contemporary opera. To allow us to experience visually the emotion of listening to the performers of an opera, the fourth cube, which highlights *Madama Butterfly*, though without neglecting the other operas selected, combines some superb historical photographs of the interpreters at the first performances with an extraordinary collection (in terms of quality and of quantity) of costume designs in oil painted by Attilio Comelli, Adolf Hohenstein, Girolamo Magnani, and Giuseppe Palanti. But opera is of course first and foremost musical theater, and so the fifth cube, *Rappresentazione*, features juxtaposed screenings of various production designs for these operas as they evolved over time, and principally of *Aida*.

The exhibition possesses one final distinguishing characteristic: it sets aside considerable space to two modern operas, Luigi Nono's *Prometeo* and Fabio Vacchi's *Teneke*, two composers who illustrate two different trends in opera and its musical language since the end of the Second World War.

Prometeo. Tragedia dell'ascolto, by Luigi Nono (1981–85)

Luigi Nono was what is called an atonal composer, that is one who does not base his music on the major or minor keys familiar for us, but on a series drawn entirely or in part from all twelve notes of the chromatic scale, C-C#-D-D#-E-F-F#, etc., each note separated from its neighbor by the narrow interval of a semitone. This system, invented at the beginning of the 20th century by Arnold Schönberg—Nono's father-in-law, coincidentally—eschews the sequence of tensions and resolutions to which we are accustomed in Western tonal music. Before the Second World War, this process had already spawned two operatic masterpieces that remain in the repertory: *Wozzeck* and *Lulu*, both by Alban Berg.

Nono's *Prometeo* (Prometheus) is thus typical of the "modernistic" current dominant in music after World War II, the most spectacular embodiment of which was the foundation of the "International Ferienkurse für Neue Musik" (summer courses in new music) at Darmstadt in southwest Germany in 1946. The music of Berio, Boulez, Cage, Nono, Pousseur, and Stockhausen (to mention just the best known) was performed there, including many world premières, while the composers provided courses and gave lectures to young students from all over the world. Nono played a central role in these courses and occupied a major position in what came to be known as the "Darmstadt School." The driving force behind these modernists was their determination to turn their backs on tradition and promote an aesthetic based on what was, at the time, regarded as progress. In the majority of cases, this musical "progressivism" went hand-in-hand with left-leaning politics and Nono himself was long a member of the Italian Communist Party, though this did not mean that a work such as *Prometeo* had to be staged as a proletarian opera—be it by conviction or imperative—as would have been the case for a Soviet composer.

Nono's modernism is manifest in his desire to forge a new kind of opera. It was not Nono's objective to construct a traditional narrative: *Prometeo* makes no effort to "tell a story"

Constructing an Opera:
The Ideas Behind an Exhibition

JEAN-JACQUES NATTIEZ

Giulio Ricordi, Giuseppe Verdi, Arrigo Boito, and his brother Camillo Boito, the architect, in front of the construction site for the rest home for elderly musicians founded by the composer • late 1890s and its libretto is the result of a collage of texts compiled by Massimo Cacciari and borrowed from texts ranging from Aeschylus to Goethe, Hölderlin, and Nietzsche up to Walter Benjamin, in Ancient Greek, Italian, and German. Neither is the opera divided into acts and scenes but, conceived as a kind of archipelago, into ten sections baptized *stasimon* (the chant of the chorus in Greek tragedy) or "*islands*." In travelling from island to island—five in number—Prometheus embodies the situation of Man as conceived by the avant-garde intelligentsia of the period. As Nono wrote: "Man and the law, Man and his continual quest for the unknown, Man and the framing of new laws and their transgression. Prometheus is Man with his eternal thirst for uncharted lands and new frontiers. It voices the revolt against the repressive powers that thwart the birth of a new era."

Such a position can be given a political twist, but it can also be seen as a description of the search of a modernist composer at odds with tradition and craving new sound horizons. As was the case with other works of the period (one thinks of *Opera* and *Sinfonia* by Berio), *Prometeo* is an invitation to reflect on the phenomenon of music itself. Its subtitle is a "tragedy of listening," and indeed some of its passages, practically inaudible, are marked *pianississimi*, if I can use such a term, a dynamic noted on the score as eight *pianos: pppppppp*. Striving to overcome the "sclerosis of habit" Nono desired "the inaudible to be made finally listenable." The drama of *Prometeo* is not that recounted on stage, but, as Jurg Stenzl, a Nono specialist, has observed, it unfolds in between the music and the listener. *Prometeo* is also modernist from the point of view of the musical resources employed: No longer are there on the one side an orchestra in its pit and on the other the singers and chorus on stage. The work is written for two groups of soloists (seven instrumentalists and five singers), a small chorus, four orchestral groups ranging from 12 to 14 musicians, each with its own conductor, all coordinated by one further conductor. Moreover, Nono calls for electronic equipment that alters the instrumental music in real time, so that the audience simultaneously hears the natural, original sound and the electronically morphed one. The sound of the instrumentalists is relayed "live" into the auditorium using an apparatus named after its inventor, the Halaphone. Albeit with modern materials, Nono here rejoins the venerable tradition of Giovanni Gabrieli, who composed his works for the enormous edifice that is St. Mark's Cathedral in Venice.

It is readily understandable that a work so remote from traditional ideas about opera calls for a theatrical realization adapted to its peculiar forces that breaks with classical production concepts. With this intention in mind, Luigi Nono called on the services of the famous architect Renzo Piano. For *Prometeo*, the designer of the Pompidou Center in Paris and the airport at Osaka came up with a kind of wooden hull measuring some 9,000 cubic meters able to contain not only the protagonists in the opera but also the audience around which the actors move. This in turn could be placed in an even vaster space—as was the case in the church of San Lorenzo in Venice for the first performance on 22 September 1984, under the baton of Claudio Abbado.

Götterdämmerung, Richard Wagner • Ricordi edition (1889)
• seen here in an exemplar printed in the early 20th century

Constructing an Opera: The Ideas Behind an Exhibition

JEAN-JACQUES NATTIEZ

Teneke by Fabio Vacchi (2007)

Very different are the aesthetics behind Fabio Vacchi's opera *Teneke*, on a libretto by Franco Marcoaldi, premièred with great success at La Scala in Milan on 22 September 2007, conducted by Roberto Abbado, directed by Ermanno Olmi, and with sets and costumes by Arnaldo Pomodoro. This work can be regarded as representative of what is today dubbed postmodernism, or sometimes "post-avant-garde," and as such it no longer seeks to challenge listeners with recourse to an exploded musical language, nor stymie them by undermining traditional dramatic structures, though this does not mean that it is divorced from the preoccupations of its time.

Inspired by an eponymous novel by Yasar Kemal (translated as *The Drumming-Out*) and classically divided into three acts and twenty-one scenes, *Teneke*, set in Turkish Anatolia in the 1950s, deals with the tensions between political power—embodied by the honest, well-meaning but inexperienced district governor, Irmaklï—and the economic clout of the local rice producers. Hell-bent on planting new and apparently more profitable paddy-fields, the latter seek seasonal concessions which, unlike traditional farming, wreak havoc on the local population and public health, flooding a village and turning it into a malarial death-trap. The opera features Irmaklï's surrender to the demands of the landowners, the flooding of the village, the peasants' revolt, the revoking of the permits, the landowners' wrath, the corruption of a number of individuals, various attempts by the women of the village to save it, all ending with the victory of the bigwigs and landowners. The poverty of the rural world and the conflict with the landowners are placed in a wider international context through the character of Nermin, the fiancée of one of the characters who challenges the extortion. She embodies the desire to unite traditional Turkey so that it can progress in step with the West, thereby bringing ideals of justice and equal rights, etc., to the country. The conclusion? Law has no value, brute force rules the world and injustice prevails; but we can only hope that this will not be forever, since defeat today can be turned into victory tomorrow and the outcome of the battle between good and evil is not a foregone conclusion. This is brought out in the score by the derisory rattle of tin drums—*teneke*—that accompanies Irmaklï as he leaves followed by all those who, with him, set off to continue the struggle for a better world elsewhere and with renewed vigor.

This dramatic story takes place in a large and complex theatrical machine of great starkness and power that splendidly conveys the deep attachment of the peasants to their sickening and infertile scrap of the earth's crust. It was designed by Arnoldo Pomodoro, a sculptor of international repute as well as a set designer for opera and the theater, known for the huge ball that stands in front of the United Nations building in New York. A remarkable collection of his works can be admired in his foundation's museum in Milan. As an example of his staging, Scene VII of Act Two presents the peasants and their animals bogged down in mud—a predicament from which the men try to escape through their revolt. Yet their struggle is to no avail, an inevitable outcome that is embodied by the whole set gradually being engulfed in water.

↑ *Ars et labor*, 1907, vol. II • Ricordi magazine founded in 1906 • Cover designed by Marcello Dudovich

"'A Vucchella," Francesco Paolo Tosti (music)/Gabriele D'Annunzio (lyrics) • Neapolitan song published by Ricordi, 1907 →

A Peppino Sirignano

'A Vucchella

(Canzone Napolétana)

Gabriele D'Annunzio

F. Paolo Tosti

Esemplare corretto per la stampa T.

Le Tapis d'orient (Il tappeto rosa), Jules Burgmein • Liège, Théâtre du Pavillon de Flore, 1912 • The Bazar • Set design by Giuseppe Palanti

Constructing an Opera:
The Ideas Behind an Exhibition

JEAN-JACQUES NATTIEZ

Fabio Vacchi's music is a far cry from the asceticism of the dodecaphonic music of the years 1945-80. Though he has abandoned the incantatory, demonstrative illusions of the modernistic period, Vacchi has not forgotten how to exploit their positive aspects, as shown in his subtle and detailed musical idiom. Moreover, he has inherited from Mahler, Ravel, and Berg, it would seem, a fine sense of orchestration. In the light of such enduring expressivity and sensitivity, it scarcely matters that this might be seen as a step backwards. Like his other works, *Teneke* is a *beautiful* piece, eloquently dramatic, often dark and tormented, but never routine. For Vacchi, a piece of music is not simply a set of abstract structures, but rather—without forfeiting rigor or construction—the manner in which a composer keen to engage with the problems of his own time interacts with his audience at the most profound level. Unlike the preceding generation, he wants to build bridges between the emotions of his listeners (and viewers) and the feelings of his characters: frustration, revolt, or hope, even love. In this, Vacchi, if in quite a different language, is simply returning to the dramatic tradition that underpins the works of the "big five" of Italian opera.

Teneke, Fabio Vacchi • Milan, Teatro alla Scala, 2007
• Page from the autograph score, Act I

a t.
♩=108
32
Fl 1 2
ott
ob 1 2
C. i
Cl. in LA 1 2
Cl. basso
2 Fg
C fg
4 Cr in FA
1.3. (SORD)
Tr in SIb 1 2,3
3 Trbn
Tuba
Wood block
Grancassa
Timpani
Campane tubolari
Triangolo
Bongos
Tamburo militare
Lion roar
ORD
div
unis.
V. ni
V. le
V. c
C. b
Fabio Vacchi (dal manoscritto di Teneke)

THE MAKING OF AN OPERA

LIBRETTO

Spoken Drama, Sung Drama:
The Preparation of Opera Librettos from ROSSINI to PUCCINI

LUCA ZOPPELLI

La bohème, Giacomo Puccini • Turin, Teatro Regio, 1896
• Cover of the printed libretto

Spoken Drama, Sung Drama:
The Preparation of Opera Librettos from ROSSINI to PUCCINI

LUCA ZOPPELLI

Although one tends to forget the libretto in the end product (it is absorbed, so to speak, in the wash of sound that is opera), it nonetheless represents an essential phase in the creation of such a work.

It is a framework with a profound impact not only on the overall meaning and dramaturgy of what is seen on stage, but also on a substantial proportion of the decisions taken by the composer as to dynamics, melody, and expression. What then were the stages in drafting a libretto in the Italian theatrical universe of the 19th and the early 20th centuries? To what extent would a publisher such as Ricordi become directly implicated in the choice of subject, its treatment, and librettist? From all these points of view, the century running from Rossini to Puccini was one of wholesale upheaval in which, as we shall see, the role of the publisher expanded to an extraordinary degree.

One question, however, needs to be addressed before we proceed: What exactly is a libretto's purpose? In fact, a casual observer might well wonder why composers never just select a dramatic text and put it to music as it stands. There were various reasons why, up until to the end of the 19th century, such an approach remained simply unthinkable. Practical conditions demanded that the plot line be pruned and the number of characters reduced. The peculiar "temporal structure" of musical drama (in which the time-flow often slows down or stops so that the emotional reactions of the protagonists can be explored) means that a script for an opera has to be far tighter than one for the spoken theater. Moreover, if certain situations are suitable for setting to music (those in which emotion predominates or a character's inner personality emerges), others are absolutely not—or only in the most unusual circumstances (such as those consisting in logical argument or prolonged debate). In brief, the action has to be clarified and made to focus on a handful of emotional cruxes or intricate situations involving only a limited cast of characters. These turning-points can then be made into musical "numbers" (introductions, finales, duets, trios, solos). Moreover, each number is organized internally in accordance with more or less obligatory forms and in particular verse types (since the length of a line and the position of its accents determine the type of melody to which it can be set). The librettist is then, so to speak, the "technician" responsible for this transformation. At the beginning of the 19th century, once he had received his assignment from a theatrical impresario, he would run through a mass of various subjects until coming across one that might easily be boiled down to an opera. He would then write a complete adaptation—occasionally conferring with the composer over basic questions—which he would then hand over to be set to music. In this period, the influence of the publisher obviously remained negligible and was usually limited to acquiring the publishing rights for an opera once it had been composed and performed to public acclaim.

La traviata, Giuseppe Verdi • First page of the printed libretto, a version censured in those cities under the control of the Papal States, Bologna, 1853 ➽

Violetta

~~LA TRAVIATA~~

~~Libretto di Francesco Maria Piave~~

MUSICA DEL MAESTRO

GIUSEPPE VERDI

CAV. DELLA LEGION D' ONORE

Milano

DALL' I. R. STABILIMENTO NAZIONALE PRIVILEG. DI

TITO DI GIO. RICORDI

Cont. degli Omenoni, N. 1720

e sotto il portico a fianco dell' I. R. Teatro alla Scala.

24282

Spoken Drama, Sung Drama:
The Preparation of Opera Librettos from ROSSINI to PUCCINI

LUCA ZOPPELLI

Over the course of the 19th century, a range of factors fostered a shift in the onus for aesthetic matters from the poet to the composer. With Gioachino Rossini, it was the composer who imposed himself in the public mind as the only true "author" of an opera, whereas previously he had been regarded as simply one of many collaborators responsible for producing the piece. It was increasingly apparent that composers were no longer satisfied with merely setting to music something already done and dusted, and that they now demanded a say as to the choice and structure of the drama. By the 1830s and '40s, therefore, the situation had become rather entangled. Masterful librettists such as Felice Romani and Salvadore Cammarano would come up with subjects whose internal logic—the situations extracted from the original drama, their arrangement, the eventual additions and alterations—had often been thrashed out first with the composer. At other times, an idea might originate with the composer himself: Gaetano Donizetti, an insatiable reader, confessed that he had various subjects "bubbling away in him" *(bollono in corpo)*. Or else a great singer might make a telling contribution: it was, for instance, the soprano Giuditta Pasta who persuaded Romani and Vincenzo Bellini to abandon *Cristina di Svezia* and take up *Beatrice di Tenda* instead. Suggestions might also be made by other protagonists in the opera world: it was the director of productions at Venice's La Fenice, Nani Mocenigo, who mentioned the subject of *Hernani* to Francesco Maria Piave and Giuseppe Verdi.

Once a subject was decided upon, a summary in prose—variously known as *piano, programma, schizzo, selva* ("plan," "program," "sketch," "rough outline")—was compiled with the purpose of parceling out the dramatic material into the various

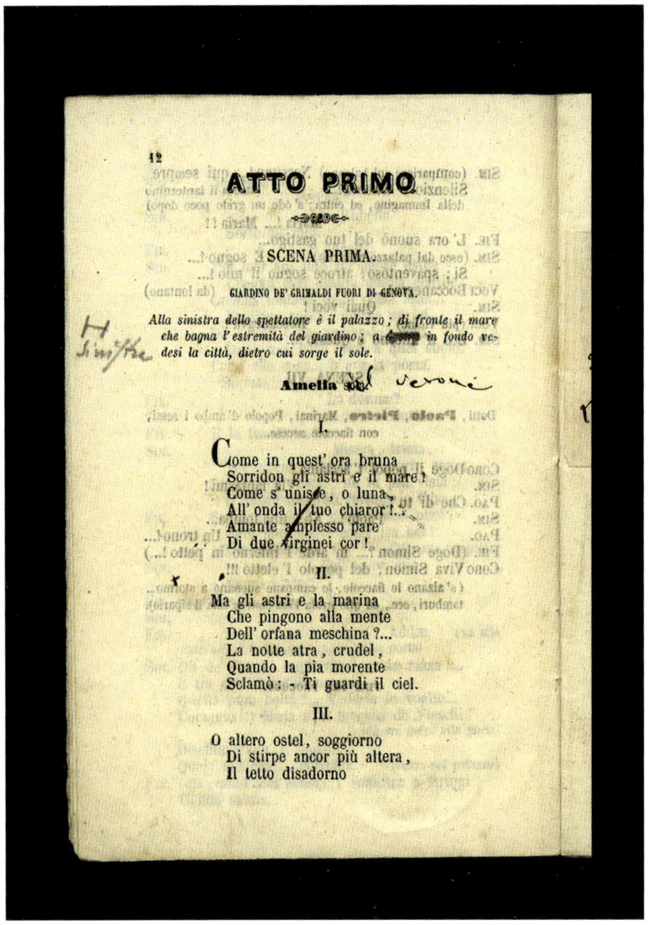

12

ATTO PRIMO

SCENA PRIMA.

GIARDINO DE' GRIMALDI FUORI DI GENOVA.

Alla sinistra dello spettatore è il palazzo; di fronte il mare che bagna l'estremità del giardino; a [illegible] in fondo vedesi la città, dietro cui sorge il sole.

Amelia [illegible]

I.

Come in quest' ora bruna
Sorridon gli astri e il mare!
Come s' unisce, o luna,
All' onda il tuo chiaror!...
Amante amplesso pare
Di due virginei cor!

II.

Ma gli astri e la marina
Che pingono alla mente
Dell' orfana meschina?...
La notte atra, crudel,
Quando la pia morente
Sclamò: - Ti guardi il ciel.

III.

O altero ostel, soggiorno
Di stirpe ancor più altera,
Il tetto disadorno

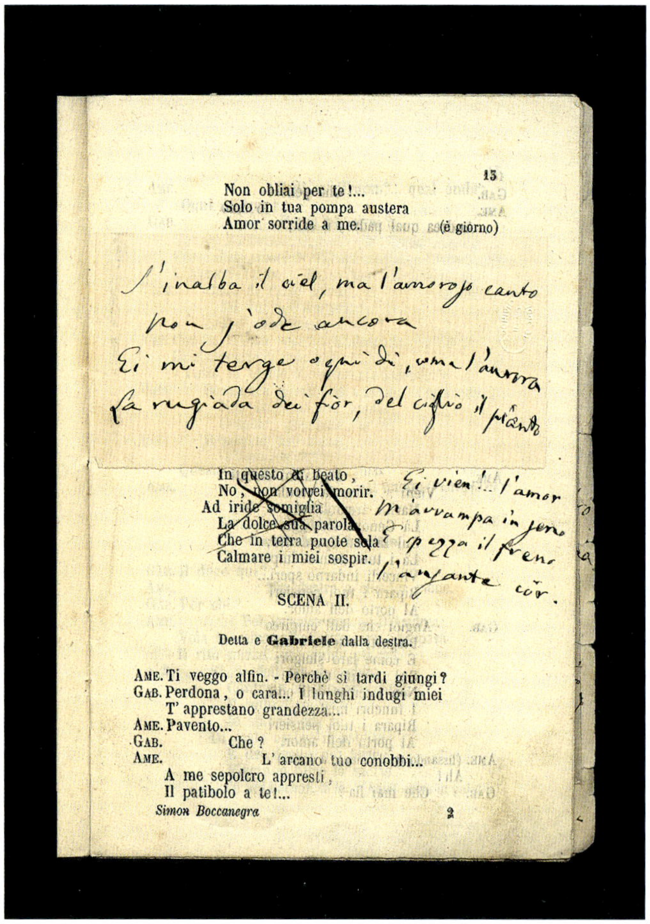

15

Non obliai per te!...
Solo in tua pompa austera
Amor sorride a me. (è giorno)

In questo dì beato,
No, non vorrei morir.
Ad iride somiglia
La dolce sua parola
Che in terra puote sola
Calmare i miei sospir.

SCENA II.

Detta e **Gabriele** dalla destra.

AME. Ti veggo alfin. - Perchè sì tardi giungi?
GAB. Perdona, o cara... I lunghi indugi miei
T' apprestano grandezza...
AME. Pavento...
GAB. Che?
AME. L' arcano tuo conobbi...
A me sepolcro appresti,
Il patibolo a te!...

Simon Boccanegra 2

Simon Boccanegra (second version), Giuseppe Verdi • Milan, Teatro alla Scala, 1881 • Printed libretto with changes by Verdi: "Come in quest'ora bruna" scenes that foreshadow the relative musical "numbers" and their structure. Duly accepted by those responsible for the opera season and provisionally approved by the political authorities, the outline was then written out completely in verse; as each act was completed it was sent off to the composer and set to music. As he proceeded, a composer might notify the poet of corrections in form or meter to be made. Right up to the eve of the performance, various contingencies—such as a singer pulling out—might necessitate still further adjustments.

As the 19th century progressed, however, this production process became increasingly problematic. Initially, the thorniest question was that of the selection of a musically pliable subject, since the source had to be at once adaptable to opera's special theatricality of the "affects," to conform to the supposedly unbreakable rules of a form of official and aristocratic entertainment, and be sufficiently familiar to whet the curiosity of audiences and maybe even supply them with a vague inkling as to the plot—something notoriously hard to get over in detail in an opera. These demands resulted in a good deal of head-scratching. In illustration, there is the story told by the librettist Jacopo Ferretti of an impromptu "crisis meeting" involving himself, Rossini, and the Roman impresario Pietro Cartoni in an effort to find a new subject after an earlier proposal had been rejected by the censor:

> That freezing evening, I came up with some twenty or thirty subjects for a melodrama, but one was thought too serious—and in Rome at least at carnival time they wanted to laugh—the next too complicated, another overly expensive for the impresario [...] and the last unsuited to the virtuosos engaged to sing it. Exhausted by all these proposals and falling half asleep, I mumbled in the midst of a yawn the word "Cendrillon" and Rossini, who, in order to concentrate better had taken to his bed, raised himself up like [the Ghibelline] Farinata in Dante['s *Inferno*], saying: "You're thinking of writing a *Cinderella* for me?" And I replied: "And you of putting it to music?" Then he: "When could you get me an outline?" Me: "...Even as tired as I am, by tomorrow morning." Rossini: "Good night."

In this case, it was the choice of subject that was arduous, but once that particular treasure had been unearthed, *Cenerentola* could be drafted in the twinkling of an eye.

As time passed, however, the problems mounted. It was no longer enough to hit upon an interesting subject—it had to be translated into a truly functioning opera. Whence did such difficulties arise? In part, from the slow demise of the apparently compulsory character of certain dramatic and formal conventions. Up until the 1840s, the cast of characters, their roles, and the vocal ranges had been governed by a handful of rigid rules: the majority of the numbers was organized, as a contemporary put it, according to a highly codified *solita forma* ("standard form"). In this sense, shortening a drama down to the length of a libretto demanded a craftsman's skill, but there were few doubts as to the formal and dramatic principles involved. Later in the period, however, composers took ever greater liberties with the form and dynamics of the events they treated, conferring greater weight on sections that would previously have been considered merely transitional, while omitting others traditionally considered sacrosanct. In short, nothing could be taken for granted and the manner in which a play might be turned into an opera had to be reconsidered on a case-by-case basis.

Behind all this, a fundamental change in the aesthetic approach of composers of Italian opera was afoot. They now conceived of the fruit of their labor no longer as a matter of skilled craftsmanship, but rather as an artwork in the loftiest sense of the term: no mere amusement, but an instance of *Weltliteratur* equal in dignity to any masterpiece of literature or the fine arts. This attitude brought with it a new-found respect for literary sources: the works of Schiller, Victor Hugo, and Shakespeare were no longer simply sources of material from which a suitable opera subject might be distilled, but great works of art of which the composers felt compelled to conserve—despite the inevitable alterations—at the very least the spirit, and even, wherever possible and for certain key moments, the original words as well. This, at root, was the underlying problem confronting Verdi and his literary collaborators.

On the one side, Verdi knew full well that spoken drama and opera obey separate laws: theatrical interest in an opera has to derive from the situation, presented in a concise, gripping way through the use of verbal pointers, avoiding the temptation of a lengthy "poetical" depiction of its ideas. Hence Verdi's constant exhortations to his librettists to stick to the point:

> In this genre of composition, there is no effect if there's no action; so keep the words to an absolute minimum! I appeal for brevity, and fire!
> Often [...] a phrase or sentence that might appear wonderful in a book and in spoken drama as well comes over as laughable in the music theater.

Spoken Drama, Sung Drama:
The Preparation of Opera Librettos from ROSSINI to PUCCINI

LUCA ZOPPELLI

Arrigo Boito and Giuseppe Verdi • Milan, 1892
• In the garden of Giulio Ricordi's house in Via Borgonuovo

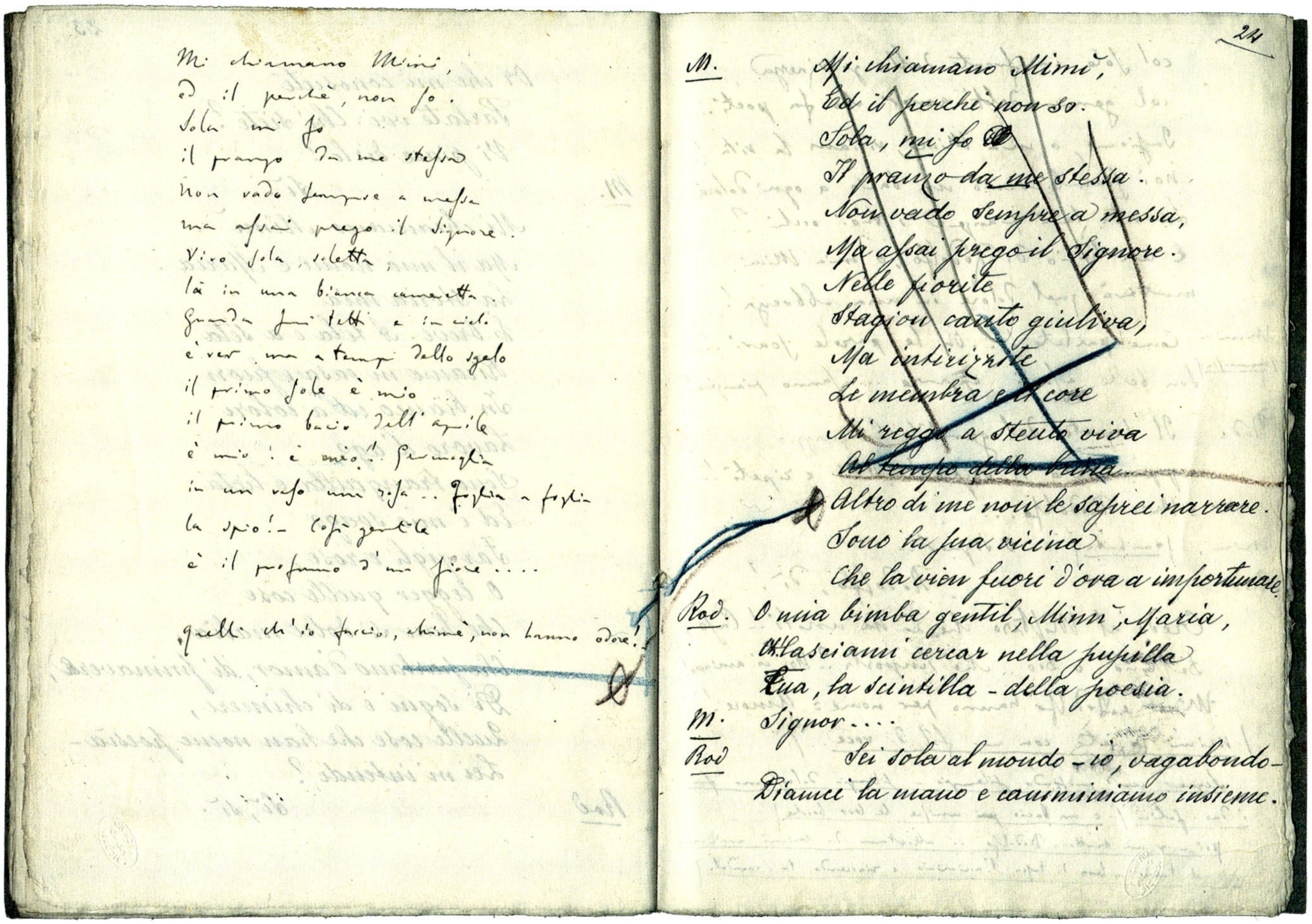

La bohème, Giacomo Puccini • Turin, Teatro Regio, 1896
• Handwritten libretto draft of Act I with notes by Puccini and the librettists
Luigi Illica and Giuseppe Giacosa

Spoken Drama, Sung Drama:
The Preparation of Opera Librettos from ROSSINI to PUCCINI

LUCA ZOPPELLI

He also believed, however, that recasting a literary model in view of an opera had to respect the personalities of the protagonists and the meaning of the play, to the point even of recycling expressions or particularly telling images from the dramatic text ("Don't forget certain really beautiful phrases in the original"). The difficulty of a reduction, therefore, lies in the miniscule room for maneuver between two contradictory impulses: faithfulness to the original, versus an anti-literary stagecraft that does not rely on the supremacy of the word but on "situations" rewritten in musical language. All in all, in distilling its "meaning," one has to partially betray the letter of the original. In Verdi's case, the process might be said to consist in getting hold of the "idea"—a sort of principle of psychology and dramaturgy from which the organic whole of the literary source springs (the concept of the curse in *Le Roi s'amuse*; the obsession with vendetta in *El Trovador*)—and only then forging the musical tools (vastly different from those employed in the spoken theater of course) with which to convey this essence. In extreme cases, this new "intellectual" standpoint would drive a composer to saddle himself with a subject not on the face of it conducive to being converted into an opera; a time-honored sense of craft might make him think twice, but his admiration for the quality of the source compelled him to make a stab at it. For Verdi, this was the case with *King Lear*, a lifetime's dream that had in the end to be dropped since the composer found the task of reconciling the demands of music drama with his respect for the original simply impossible to resolve.

From this novel situation there hatched a wholly new hierarchy: librettists now became mere helpmates striving to realize the theatrical intentions of the composer, the latter having extracted the quintessential "meaning" of the piece. Indeed, in the event of the two parties failing to see eye to eye, and if the librettist possessed sufficient sway and experience to hold his own against the composer, things could become stormy—as with Verdi and Cammarano in writing *Il trovatore*. Practically, and on the contractual level, these changes corresponded to a new pattern of relationships: a composer such as Verdi would henceforth avoid selling his operas to a theater for a one-off payment; preserving ownership, he now had simply to find a publisher with whom to manage it. As the sole proprietor of the opera—and, as such, sole guarantor of its aesthetic authority—henceforth it would be his task to pay the librettist for services rendered. The contractual relations arising between composer and publisher had r epercussions therefore on the professional status of the librettist: at this juncture the latter depended directly on the composer and no longer benefited from independent contact with the publisher.

Now the moment dawned: at the end of the 1860s, when it came to rewriting and staging the La Scala première of *La forza del destino*—already composed for St. Petersburg in 1862—the collaborator employed was in fact a man from Ricordi's circle: all-round writer, journalist, and one-time singer, the Lombard Antonio Ghislanzoni, who had also served as editor of the *Gazzetta musicale di Milano*, the house journal. Couched more or less in the following language, the correspondence dealing with the adjustments required thus passed through the office of Tito I and Giulio Ricordi:

> Get Ghislanzoni to find a *sdrucciolo* [a word accented on the third-to-last syllable] instead of *perdonato* [...] and then to turn a beautiful line in place of *a te lode o Signor!* and the *coupe* [caesura] will go splendidly. He should try to find me a long syllable (if possible) as in *perdonato*. These seem trifles, but Ghislanzoni, who was once a singer, knows full well that a single syllable can sometimes ensure and sometimes spoil an effect [...].

The collaboration with Ghislanzoni touching up *La forza* was a prelude to the much more onerous task of *Aida*. In truth, Ghislanzoni's contribution seemed at the beginning as though it would be relatively secondary, limited to issues of prosody, since Verdi had agreed to set an already written subject accepted by the patrons. In his opinion, the outline, penned by the Egyptologist Auguste Mariette, seemed "well made," "splendidly theatrical," and featuring a few situations which, "if not of the newest, [are] truly beautiful." It was to Giulio Ricordi that the composer turned for contact with a librettist:

> I have an exhaustive plan for an opera, complete with characters, choruses, *mise en scène*, act divisions, etc. All that's missing is the dialog and the poetry. If I were to make an opera out of it, could Ghislanzoni write me the libretto? Explain to him that it is not original work; the task is simply to compose the verse, which, it should be clearly understood this I can tell you), will be very generously remunerated.

From these lines the impression transpires that Verdi reckoned that the task awaiting Ghislanzoni would be of an uncomplicated and essentially mechanical nature. We know though that things did not fall out quite like this: although the general plan of the libretto had already been established, the precise relationships between the protagonists and their motives—let alone the attendant issues of form and meter—still demanded an immense amount of work as some of the most famous passages in Verdi's correspondence bear witness. On the one hand, the composer made the point with his usual observations on the necessity of making the idea or the emotional crux of a given situation clear by means of transparent and well-constructed expressions, often complaining that the straitjacket of literary form seemed to sap the heart of the drama:

> It seems to me likewise that the *parola scenica* just isn't there—or if it is, it's buried beneath the rhyme or the verse, and therefore doesn't jump out at one as boldly and straightforwardly as it should [...]. I don't know if I make myself clear with the term *parola scenica*, but I mean those words that fashion a situation, that render it obvious to all. As an example [...], the lines:
>
> *Per Radames d'amore*
> *Ardo e mi sei rivale.*
> *– Che? Voi l'amate? – Io l'amo*
> *E figlia son d'un re*
>
> ["I burn for love of Radames and you are my rival." "What? You love him?" "I love him and am the daughter of a king."] seem less theatrical to me than the words: *"Tu l'ami? ma l'amo anch'io intendi? La figlia dei faraoni è tua rivale!"–Aida: "Mia rivale? E sia: anch'io son figlia" etc.*
> ["You love him? But I love him too, understand? The daughter of the pharaoh is your rival!" "My rival? So be it: I too am the daughter, etc."]
>
> I realize you'll reply: "What about the verse, the rhyme, the stanzas?" I don't know what to say; but for me, when the action demands it, I would immediately jettison rhythm, rhyme, and verse form. I'd use free verse so as to get over loud and clear everything the action requires. The fact is that, for the theater, poets and composers sometimes have to show their talent by leaving off both poetry and music.

On the other hand, he constantly struggled to get the poet to use a more fluent, more elastic meter, one less slave to the repetitive and restrictive confines of the Italian tradition of libretto writing:

> These two solos, even making two separate cantilenas, would be of more or less the same form, the same character; and there we fall into the commonplace. The French, even in strophic song, sometimes use longer or shorter lines. Why shouldn't we do the same? [...] A somewhat unusual verse form for Radames would oblige me to try out a melody distinct from those usually written for the *settenari* or *ottonari*, and would also force me to change pace and time signature when doing Aida's solo (a sort of half-aria).

Giacomo Puccini (left) and the librettists Giuseppe Giacosa and Luigi Illica
• circa 1896

Spoken Drama, Sung Drama: The Preparation of Opera Librettos from ROSSINI to PUCCINI

LUCA ZOPPELLI

It's not that poor Ghislanzoni was more obtuse than many of his colleagues. It is rather that, with the passing years, Verdi had become more demanding and resistant to certain poetic "templates" whose hallowed strictures would imprison a now more flexible, unpredictable, fluctuating musical imagination inclined to veer between various writing styles and shifting the relationship between voice and orchestra. This hurdle—compounded by the difficulty of attaining a balance between techniques of libretto writing and a respect for the literary values of his sources—explains in part the crisis that affected Verdi in the 1870s, and his prolonged refusal to return to composing opera scores. Who could provide him with the kind of libretti he dreamed of? Faced with such problems, the respectable craft of a "minor" man of letters cobbling together a standard text for an opera was no longer going to be up to the mark.

It was at this juncture that, conceptually speaking, Giulio Ricordi took a decisive step. He possessed a "stable" with some real "thoroughbreds" (Verdi, Amilcare Ponchielli, a few years later, Giacomo Puccini): his interests as an entrepreneur, like those of every art lover, demanded that every now and then such composers bring forth an opera capable of capturing the public imagination, of filling the theaters, as well as of resonating with the opinion of cultivated audiences and satisfying the taste of the "new" but rapidly expanding petit-bourgeoisie. Yet no one needed to tell this cultured and thoughtful intellectual how thoroughbreds like those were not disposed to "run" without offering them a culturally viable and at the same time theatrically effective libretto capable of stimulating their dramatic appetite, yet malleable enough to allow them free rein as to melodic invention. This called for collaborators possessed of the highest literary ability but prepared, nonetheless, to take on a subordinate role. Moreover, a large network of relationships from the intellectual milieu also had to be assembled and maintained: a composer, however prestigious, cannot hope to do all this unaided. So it was that Casa Ricordi took on the task of doing it for him, to the best of its ability smoothing the path for the creation of new masterpieces thanks to the painstaking preparation of everything concerning the libretto.

The first and most illustrious outcome of this strategy is obviously the relationship that coalesced between Verdi and Arrigo Boito, an enterprise that needed patience and shrewdness, since Verdi still harbored misgivings about certain "modernist" tendencies Boito had embraced in his headstrong, bohemian years. A sensitive man of letters and a composer in his own right, Boito would have understood the hindrances that might affect another composer, above all in the area of metric structure, and discreetly informed Ricordi of his own conviction that certain technical tricks (a "specific rhythmical construction" which, he thought, would "interest our *maestro* hugely") might well constitute "a powerful spur to the realization of a plan so dear to our heart." This "plan," it goes almost without saying, was *Otello*. Knowing how committed Verdi was to it deep down, Ricordi now mildly twisted the reluctant composer's arm, practically forcing him to peruse a first draft and setting up an initial meeting. Indeed, even pastries were marshaled in this charm offensive, with Verdi taking delivery of some chocolate cakes in an allusion to the Moor of Venice, though the plan was still top secret at the time. The actual meeting proved a success; though very different in age, culture, and aesthetic background, Verdi and Boito pooled their disparate but complementary talents. The modern and "decadent" man of letters graciously took on a subsidiary role dedicated to crafting a totally Verdian dramaturgy, stating: "If I have indeed managed to intuit the singular musical potential of Shakespearian tragedy to which I had previously been insensitive, and if I have been able to demonstrate this in my libretto, it is solely because I have looked at it from the standpoint of the art of a Verdi." At the same time, thanks to his tact and undeniable intellectual appeal, Boito also succeeded in skillfully teasing out the avant-garde composer that Verdi, fundamentally, always had been, but which he had refused to demonstrate overtly due to his reservations regarding the aesthetic preciousness of modernist theories—a situation still more self-evident in his *Falstaff*.

For Puccini too, a generation later, the choice and treatment of the subject remained a thorny question and a source of much procrastination and change of heart. Giulio Ricordi, having taken on such an active role in procuring a worthwhile collaborator to work with Verdi on his masterpieces, extended and intensified his strategy for the new "thoroughbreds" of the publishing house. The case of *Manon Lescaut* is well known: the subject, which Puccini had long pondered and puzzled over, was first entrusted to Ruggero Leoncavallo, a man blessed with abilities both as a writer and a musician who Ricordi thought might turn out to be a second Boito. A host of difficulties, however, meant that the publisher had subsequently to turn to other pens, such as those of Marco Praga, Domenico Oliva, and, above all, the much-vaunted dramatist Giuseppe Giacosa, as well as to a writer who had already tried his hand at libretti, Luigi Illica. The genesis of the libretto of *Manon Lescaut* had therefore a checkered history, yet from this "laboratory" Giulio Ricordi emerged with a winning formula: a duo formed of Illica (with his extraordinary flair for a theme, his dramatic instinct, and his scene-setting abilities) and Giacosa (a literary mind of singular acuity, above all as to the treatment of the poetic "outer layer"). Unlike with Verdi and Boito,

Advertisement in the *Gazzetta musicale di Milano* • 13 December 1891 ➛
• Ricordi declares to have acquired the rights to the composition of an opera based upon Victorien Sardou's drama *La Tosca*

Gazzetta Musicale di Milano

ANNO XLVI. — DIRETTORE — FOGLIO DI 16 PAGINE

N. 50. — 13 Dicembre 1891 — GIULIO RICORDI — Si pubblica ogni Domenica

CONCERTI

MILANO. — *Società del Quartetto. — Secondo Concerto del Quartetto di Francoforte.* — Quale successo domenica e quanto godimento vero, intenso per il pubblico!

Il secondo concerto del Quartetto di Francoforte ha avuto sopratutto una felissima fisonomia di serenità.

Un programma simile, diciamolo francamente, non capita tutti i giorni; il più delle volte pare che i concertisti vadano a bella posta a cercare tutto quanto vi ha di più astruso nel loro repertorio e sembrano lieti, appagati che alla noia del pubblico si contrapponga l'entusiasmo dei critici, i quali trovano sempre il modo di farsi credere superiori d'intelligenza e capaci solo essi di comprendere ciò che la gente grossa non comprende!

Questa volta, mantenendo un programma elettissimo, è avvenuto proprio che il pubblico s'è divertito, s'è commosso, s'è entusiasmato.

Il *Quartetto* in *re minore* di Mozart, è una di quelle opere geniali, fresche della più bella gioventù del fecondo compositore, tedesco di origine, ma italiano, italianissimo nell'indole della sua musica, pari nello stile, nella fisonomia al Paisiello, al Cimarosa, allo Zingarelli e al Rossini che ne raccolse l'eredità prodigiosa! Noi, provando emozioni dolcissime allo svolgersi incessante di quelle schiette e serene melodie, e vedendo mal celato il godimento intenso dell'uditorio, ci siamo confortati, e una volta di più abbiamo avuto ragione di ritenere giuste le nostre credenze in fatto di musica. L'*Allegro moderato* e l'*Andante* avevano già conquistato il generale applauso, ma il *Minuetto* con quel *trio* smagliante d'una italianità spiccatissima, finì per infondere in tutta la sala un elettrizzante rapimento; furono viste parecchie centinaia di teste accompagnare quel vezzosissimo *ritmo* di notine legate a due a due, ma non sappiamo davvero quale specie di critico oserebbe ancora fare un addebito di ciò che rappresenta il più bel successo della bell'arte dei suoni!

Dopo il Mozart avemmo la fortuna di udire il nuovo lavoro del Bazzini, un *Pezzo di concerto* per violoncello con accompagnamento d'orchestra, pagina di molto valore, meravigliosa per vigore, per coloriti orchestrali, per ispirazione; davvero che udendo tanta freschezza e tanta potenza c'era da farsi l'illusione di una mente creatrice e d'una mano fattrice giovanissima, e per poco non sorprese il veder comparire, dopo gli applausi interminabili, il venerando Bazzini, più giovane nella sua tarda età di tanti giovani intisichiti a vent'anni!

Il pezzo, egregiamente eseguito dal violoncellista Becker e dall'orchestra guidata magistralmente dal prof. Guglielmo Andreoli, fu bissato dalla seconda parte, lasciando in tutto il pubblico una impressione di meraviglia e il desiderio che il Bazzini tragga profitto di questo suo bel momento produttivo per dare all'arte nuove gemme.

Mozart tornò col suo *Adagio* a inebbriarci, a conquiderci; a quelle note squisitamente sublimi parve spargersi per la sala un profumo di fiorita primavera; in quel momento come erano in ribasso i sermonisti delle *nebulosità!* E manco male che la colpa era di un tedesco!

Il prof. Heermann suonò l'*Adagio* da pari suo, cioè stupendamente.

Il Beethoven, quello della prima maniera, il Beethoven nella pienezza del suo sterminato genio, nella preponderanza della sua turbinosa gioventù, col *Quintetto*, op. 29, mantenne caldo l'ambiente e coronò un concerto che avrà il pregio di non esser dimenticato, come ebbe quello di aver fatto veramente divertire, d'esser sembrato breve, d'averci fatto provare tutte quelle emozioni che solo la musica può e deve far provare alla gente.

Il Quartetto Heermann-Becker eseguì tutto con una finezza, uno slancio, un *entrain* speciali; pareva che quegli esimî professori avessero capito che era un concerto indovinato, e furono in compenso applauditi con entusiasmo.

Il prof. Andreoli prese parte nel *Quintetto* di Beethoven, colla viola.

Nel pubblico, ammiratissimi, tre principi dell'arte: Rubinstein, Piatti e Boito, e nelle prime sedie la Stolz in compagnia di una signora che fece per qualche tempo sperare la presenza del re... dell'arte italiana! La signora Giuseppina Verdi, vogliamo dire; ma il maestro lasciò che lo desiderassimo!...

E siamo usciti dal Conservatorio commossi e non abbiamo saputo resistere all'impulso di entrare in quella

Spoken Drama, Sung Drama:
The Preparation of Opera Librettos from ROSSINI to PUCCINI

LUCA ZOPPELLI

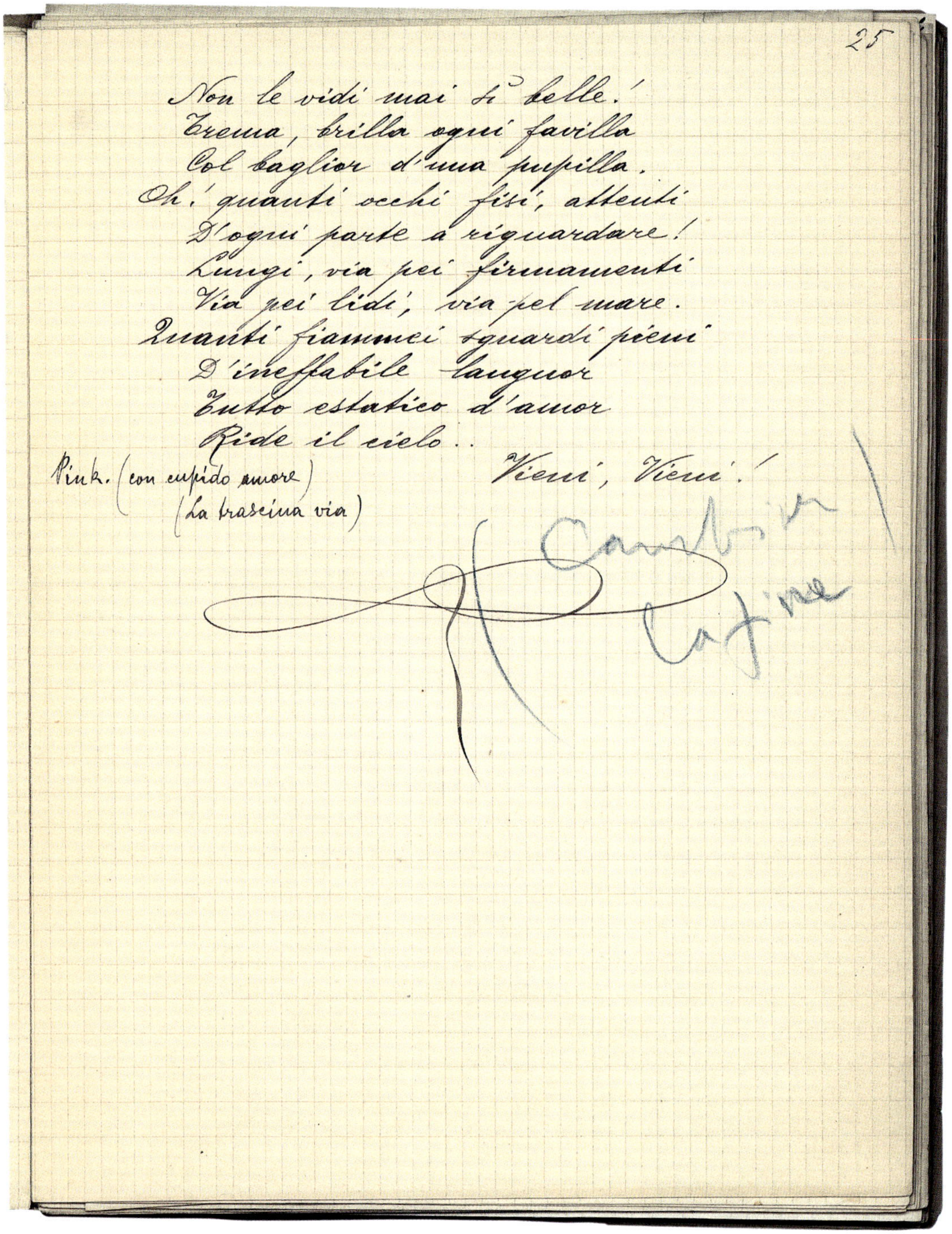
25

Non le vidi mai sì belle!
Trema, brilla ogni favilla
Col baglior d'una pupilla.
Oh! quanti occhi fisi, attenti
D'ogni parte a riguardare!
Lungi, via pei firmamenti
Via pei lidi, via pel mare.
Quanti fiammei sguardi pieni
D'ineffabile languor
Tutto estatico d'amor
Ride il cielo..
Vieni, Vieni!
Pink. (con cupido amore)
(La brascina via)
Cambia la fine

Madama Butterfly, Giacomo Puccini • Milan, Teatro alla Scala, 1904
• Handwritten libretto with corrections by Puccini and the librettist Giuseppe Giacosa, finale Act I

Guarda: è notte serena!
guarda: dorme ogni cosa!
Butt. (estatica) Dolce notte! Quante stelle!
non le vidi mai sì belle;
trema, brilla ogni favilla
col baglior d'una pupilla.
Oh! quanti occhi fisi, attenti
d'ogni parte a riguardare!
Lungi, via pei firmamenti
via pei lidi, via pel mare
~~quanti sguardi fiammeggianti!~~
~~quante vite palpitanti!~~
~~(oppressa dal turbamento per tanta bellezza ed illanguidita dall'amore si ritrae nella casa, dicendo a Pinkerton)~~
~~Chiuda – non reggo più~~
~~Pink. (cupido, all'orecchio, con voce ardente)~~
~~Dammi del tu – dammi del tu~~
~~piccola Butterfly~~ soave incanto
~~Butt (abbandonandosi tutta nelle braccia di Pinkerton)~~
~~Ti voglio bene, tesoro! (lo bacia)~~
Quanti fiammei sguardi pieni
D'ineffabile languor
Tutto estatico d'amor
Ride il cielo.
Pink. (con cupido amore) Vieni – Vieni
(~~La trascina via~~)

Spoken Drama, Sung Drama:
The Preparation of Opera Librettos from ROSSINI to PUCCINI

LUCA ZOPPELLI

in this case not only did the team have to be constituted, but the work demanded constant egging along. The two literati were often exasperated, not only because of Puccini's ceaseless requests for alterations that would be functional to the musical arrangement, but also due to the essentially "anti-literary" character of the metrical devices Puccini required; at every turn, egos had to be massaged, troubled waters calmed, and problems resolved. One can well understand therefore why, at the end of what was a huge collective effort, Giulio Ricordi said of the next opera born from the collaboration between Illica, Giacosa, and Puccini, *La bohème*: "To me it seems that [...] she is, if not quite like a daughter, then at least something of a goddaughter."

A somewhat closer scrutiny of the genesis of *Tosca* demonstrates the panoply of roles Ricordi was now expected to take on. In 1889, after seeing a performance of Victorien Sardou's play starring Sarah Bernhardt, Puccini requested Ricordi to "undertake the necessary practical steps to obtain permissions" from the author. Once the rights had been secured (at a high price, since Sardou was a fearsome negotiator), Puccini's interest seemed to wane and he became preoccupied with other projects. So much so in fact that the publisher ended up offering the subject to another composer from his stable, Alberto Franchetti, whose recent *Cristoforo Columbo* had given a new lease on life to the Italian form of *Grand-opéra* on historico-political subjects (with a marked anti-clerical twist). This was a recipe that might well work for *Tosca* also—as long as the subject was tackled in the manner of a Sardou rather than in that of a Puccini. It was therefore with Franchetti in mind that Illica started cutting down the play—until, faced with the growing perplexity of the composer as to the subject ("I had to give it up because I couldn't get a feel for the music"), in 1895 Ricordi once again dispatched the libretto to Puccini.

At this point, it fell to Giacosa to transform Illica's outline into a more extensive draft. The great dramatist, however, ran into severe difficulties, declaring the subject "absolutely unsuited" to "music theater," with too many duet scenes, an all too "mechanical" storyline, and action that "undermined the verse." In order to get the playwright to stick to the task Ricordi had to bang the table, even threatening penalties for each day over the deadline. It was then the turn of Puccini to request and introduce the customary revisions as he set the draft to music, in particular after discussing the finale with Sardou in Paris. Illica had envisaged a sort of "mad scene" for Tosca on Cavaradossi's corpse, but the two agreed that it should end in a more synthetic and abrupt manner. Once again, therefore, the final libretto was the result of a protracted to-and-fro, of a veritable joint venture driven by the sometimes uncompromising practical support and encouragement of Giulio Ricordi—though of course, in the final analysis, it was Puccini's dramatic instinct that created the strategies necessary for turning a subject judged "unsuited to music theater" into an operatic masterpiece.

Finally, it is well to recall that as the 20th century dawned, another, hitherto unprecedented possibility presented itself to composers in quest of an opera libretto: that of setting to music a preexisting dramatic text written for the spoken stage without imposing on it the forms and meter of a true libretto, but at most by making a few cuts—as is the case with Debussy's *Pelléas et Mélisande* and Strauss's *Salome*. This type of treatment—*Literaturoper*, in musicological jargon—grew to be feasible due to the fact that the sung line–syllabic, more supple in its phrasing, and adhering more closely to the action—seemed less and less to call for conventional forms and verse structures, and could now be applied to a literary text that had not been conceived in musical terms. In Italian opera of the early 20th century, this phenomenon arose essentially from the prestige enjoyed by the plays of Gabriele d'Annunzio and the possibilities they offered composers, seconded by attempts to arouse public interest and ennoble opera as a genre by resorting to poetical texts of a high literary caliber. Casa Ricordi also actively promoted operations of this type, though they first and foremost necessitated acquiring performance rights from an author scarcely less combative as regards money matters than Sardou had been. Still, it was not invariably just a question of funding: Tito II, on the point of taking over the reins of the company, personally intervened to trim down and make alterations to d'Annunzio's *Francesca da Rimini* in view of the opera (1914) destined to launch a new arrival in Casa Ricordi's stable, Riccardo Zandonai. Tito's intervention consisted above all in pitilessly weeding out a substantial proportion of the elaborate imagism and verbal and poetical acrobatics from d'Annunzio's text. This was a doubtful operation at best, since—like them or not—they constitute the linchpin of d'Annunzio's conception of the theater. Nonetheless his work gave rise to a passably effective musical drama, to the point indeed that *Francesca da Rimini*, unique among its composer's scores and among all the *Literaturopern* based on texts by d'Annunzio, has enjoyed a successful career on the international stage over the course of the century and is occasionally reprised even today.

Occurring on the eve of the First World War, this episode is possessed of symbolic value: if, in the course of the "Ricordi century," the active role of the publisher in creating a libretto had grown enormously, *Francesca da Rimini* saw it flower into veritable co-authorship of the plan and text of the poem.

Tosca, Giacomo Puccini • Rome, Teatro Costanzi, 1900
• Manuscript libretto draft with notes by Puccini

Sì

(non l'ho impiegato perchè antipatico)

Scarpia che cede. ~~A qual prezzo?~~ La prim
Sua grazia è questa....

Tosca — e l'ultima!

Cav — Che dic

Tosca — Il tuo sangue o il mio amore
volea. Fur vani scongiuri e pianti
Invan, pazza d'orrore
alla Madonna mi volsi ed ai Santi....
Rideva - il mostro! - del mio martir!
Dicea già negli oscuri
cieli il patibol le braccia leva!
Rullavano i tamburi......
Rideva, l'empio mostro.... rideva...
già la sua preda pronto a ghermir!
«Sei mia?» - Sì - Alla sua brama
mi promisi. Lì presso
luccicava una lama....
Ei scrisse il foglio liberator,
venne all'orrendo amplesso....
Io quella lama gli piantai nel cor

Cav — Tu?!... di tua man l'uccidesti! - tu pia
tu benigna e per me!

Tosca — N'ebbi le mani
tutte lorde di sangue!..

Cav — (prendendo amorosamente fra le sue le mani di Tosca

PARTITURA

From Words to Music:
Libretto, Score, Stagecraft: The Process in VERDI

PIERLUIGI PETROBELLI

I lombardi alla prima crociata, Giuseppe Verdi • Cover of the vocal score, 1878: seen here in an exemplar printed in 1882

e pure quanti gruppi

Così pure per le

From Words to Music:
Libretto, Score, Stagecraft: The Process in VERDI

PIERLUIGI PETROBELLI

For Verdi, actually writing the score—in the sense of creating the musical component of an opera with both the sung lines and the orchestral parts—did not mark the start of the creative trajectory, but its end point.

Only once the composer was totally convinced of the dramatic and verbal structure of the text for which he was to compose the music did he apply himself to the task of creating the score. Highly revealing in this connection is a letter Verdi sent to the president of the Teatro la Fenice of Venice on 24 August 1850, when the suspicion was in the air that the censor might prohibit the subject of *Le Roi s'amuse* chosen for the opera that became *Rigoletto.*

> The notion that *Le Roi s'amuse* might not be permitted places me in a serious quandary. I was assured by [Francesco Maria] Piave [at this time "the poet" of the Teatro La Fenice] that the subject would present no obstacle and I, trusting in your poet, set to studying and thinking about it deeply, and the idea, the musical color had formed in my mind. I can safely say that for me the bulk of the job was done. If I were now obliged to treat a different subject, I would not have enough time to undertake such study again and I could not, in all conscience, hope to write another work to my satisfaction.

Glaring further proof of this fundamental prerequisite for Verdi's creativity is provided by his fruitless forty-year struggle to compose an opera on Shakespeare's *King Lear.* The first hints concerning this literary and dramatic text appear in his correspondence as early as 1843; the divers, amply documented attempts to work with librettists were pursued primarily in the years between 1850 and 1856, at first with Salvadore Cammarano and then with Antonio Somma. Once again in 1864 and perhaps during the last decade of his life, Verdi returned at least in thought to this subject, but we have reason to conclude—if for no other reason than for its protracted gestation—that Verdi never reached the stage of musical composition.

From this point of view, as in other ways, Verdi's approach constitutes a decisive break with the typical practice of composing Italian opera in the early 19th century. If Rossini has been described—with some exaggeration and in all likelihood apocryphally—as being "indifferent" to the dramatic and verbal structure of whatever he set to music, for Donizetti and above all for Bellini the interest was centered on the words, on the diction of the theatrical incident, whereas the unfolding of the drama, and still more the concatenation of the various events, were treated as subordinate. If on more than one occasion these composers happened to write dramatically powerful and unified scores, this occurred more thanks to their theatrical instinct than to any conscious engagement with a dramatic conception. With a composer like Verdi, the situation was wholly different.

Giuseppe Verdi • sitting in the garden of Giulio Ricordi's house in Via Borgonuovo, Milan, 1892

From Words to Music:
Libretto, Score, Stagecraft: The Process in VERDI

PIERLUIGI PETROBELLI

La traviata, Giuseppe Verdi • Autograph musical sketch for Act 1

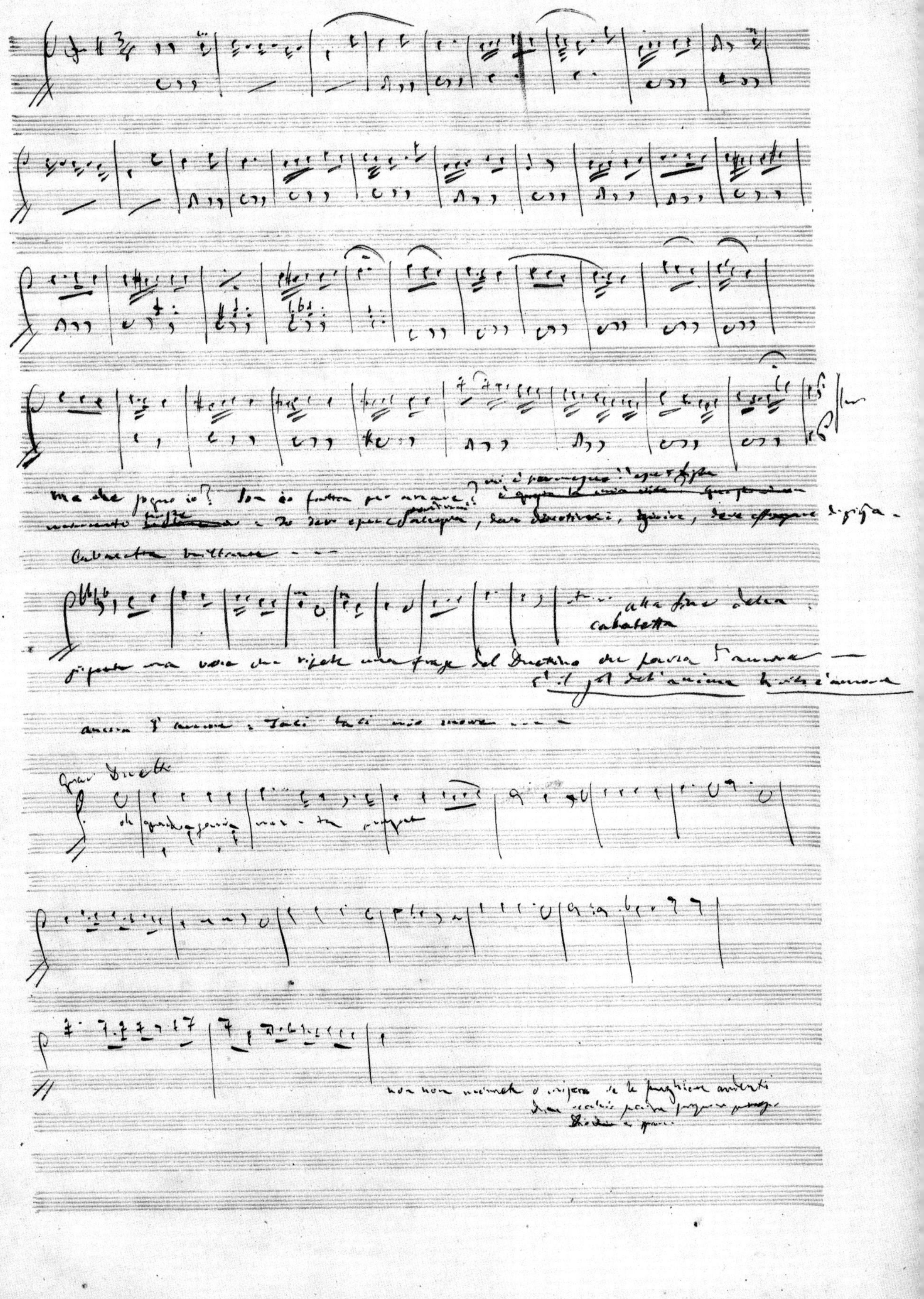
Ma che sogno io? Son io fatta per amare?
Cabaletta brillante
alla fine della cabaletta
Gran Duetto

From Words to Music: Libretto, Score, Stagecraft: The Process in VERDI

PIERLUIGI PETROBELLI

A further fundamental document for understanding Verdi's creative method is the initial draft for the entire first act of *Traviata*. This draft is almost certainly contemporary, or immediately subsequent to, Verdi's rapid decision (one that put all previous plans on hold) to set Alexandre Dumas *fils' Dame aux camélias* to music, taken at the end of September or beginning of October 1852. In this draft the succession of events on stage is explicitly noted down in words: the entrance of the guests for the party, the banquet, the opening of the dialog between "Margherita" and the "tenor," the departure of the guests, the grand aria of the main character that closes the act. Yet for only two episodes did the composer sketch out the music: the "brindisi" (toast) by the tenor, subsequently taken up by the other voices; and the beginning of the two-part (cantabile and cabaletta) aria ending the act. In this initial phase of composition, then, dramatic articulation of the episodes still prevails over musical invention. That this exceptional document exists stems from the fact that, for the opera that will become *La traviata*, Verdi did not have sufficient time to "study" or "ponder" the matter deeply and elaborate an orderly musical development, and so was unable to draft a sketch of the entire score. When time and circumstances permitted, he would lay out on music paper each and every event in the action, from the first to the last bar, focusing on the development of the vocal parts and the instrumental bass line, and only sporadically jotting in a harmonic progression or indications of orchestral color. This is the technique of a "continuity draft," a compositional approach that fosters, on the level of musical language, the creation of a poetics of dramatic unity and for which we have examples from Verdi's operas in an almost unbroken line from *Luisa Miller* (1849) through *Falstaff* (1893).

Verdi intended the musical development of the action to unfold consistently from beginning to end such that each instant would lead inexorably toward the concluding *katastrophé*. Dramatic pace therefore emerges directly in musical terms as a rhythm born from an alternation of stasis (that is of unitary, "closed" pieces: airs, duets, choruses, ensembles) and concentrated flurries of action, without, however, there invariably being a clean break between these two poles of dramatic flow. In this perspective, maximum importance is assigned to the duration of each single incident, because it is from the relationship between them that the dramatic impetus springs.

It is therefore no coincidence that in Verdi's correspondence with librettists—and this, from his earliest operas—there appear with almost obsessive insistence appeals for brevity: "Very, very, very few words!!!" This is because it is from the choice of just the right word or phrase, which can characterize and clarify a dramatic situation, that the composer can forge a distinct musical identity. Telling in this respect is another passage in the correspondence, this time with the librettist of *Aida*, the untried Antonio Ghislanzoni, to whom Verdi found himself obliged to explain his ideas and demands time and time again. It is worth quoting the beginning of a letter of 17 August 1870, regarding the second-act duet between the two rival women, Amneris and Aida:

> At the beginning and at the end of the duet there are fine things, but it is too long and drawn out. It seems to me that the recitative could be expressed in fewer verses. The stanza is good until "*a te in cor destò*." But when later on the action heats up, it appears to me that the *parola scenica* just isn't there. I don't know if I make myself clear with the term *parola scenica*, but I mean those words that define a situation, that render it clear and obvious to all. For example, the lines:
>
> *In volto gli occhi affissami*
> [Fix your eyes on my face]
>
> *E menti ancor se l'osi –*
> [And lie again, if you dare –]
>
> *Radames vive …*
> [Radames lives…]
>
> are less theatrically effective than the words
> (which you may think are ugly):
>
> *… con una parola*
> [With a single word]
>
> *strapperò il tuo segreto.*
> [I'll expose your secret]
>
> *Guardami t'ho ingannata:*
> [Look at me, I've tricked you:]
>
> *Radames vive …*
> [Radames lives …]

Verdi is first and foremost a man of the theater (this explains the enduring presence of his works, still today, in opera houses the world over). Composers and librettists alike must on occasion bow to the exigencies of stagecraft; as he says in the same letter to Ghislanzoni: "The fact is that, for the theater, poets and composers sometimes have to show their talent by leaving off both poetry and music."

In the opera house, audiences use their ears, but they also use their eyes. Therefore—still against the background of a poetics of dramatic unity—the musical aspect and its counterpart, the onstage business, possess equal importance. This too was a radically new concept in the history of Italian opera and it is symptomatic that Verdi returns time and again to this theatrical component in his correspondence. At the period of the première of *Falstaff* as well, the composer discussed with his publisher Ricordi—who was acting as go-between with the set designer and with the Teatro alla Scala where the opera was to open—the staging of two episodes in the opera: the second scene of the first act in the garden at Ford's house, and the second part of the second act in the reception room of the same residence. Things reached such a pitch that, so as to make his intentions crystal clear, in a letter of 18 September 1892 the composer even sketched a brief layout of the scene:

> You had a few questions about the actors' *entrances* and *exits*. Nothing could be simpler or easier than this *mise en scène* as long as the designer does the set just as I envisaged it when I wrote the music. Nothing more than a large, authentic garden, with avenues, clusters of bushes, and plants here and there so that one can hide, appear, and disappear as desired whenever this is required by the drama and music. In this way, the men have their own separate area and can invade that of the women whenever the latter are not on stage. And the women too can, at the end of the act, take over the space previously occupied by the men. Don't tell anyone anything about these scrawls of mine (not even Boito), just keep an eye on the ideas of Hohenstein [the set designer] to see if they more or less coincide with mine.

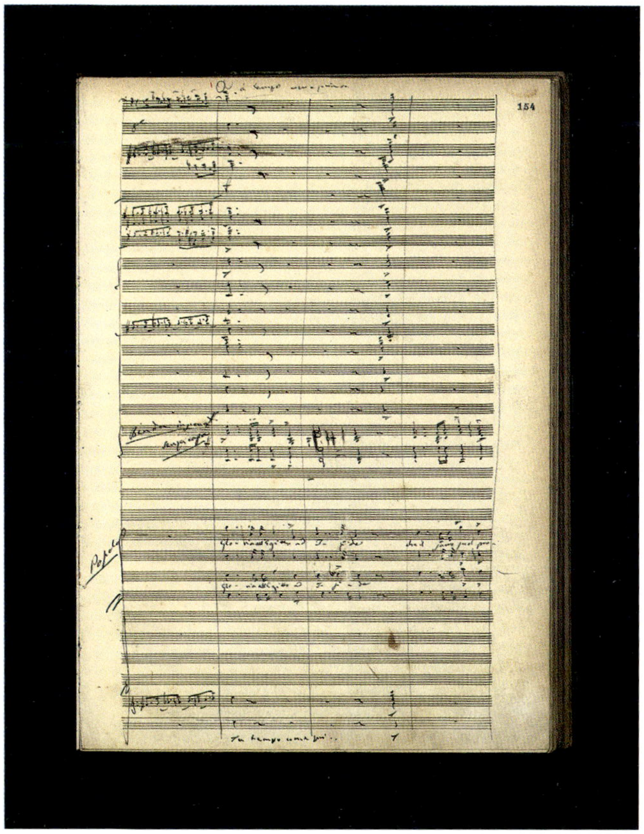

Aida, Giuseppe Verdi • Autograph score, 1871
• the Triumphal March

From Words to Music:
Libretto, Score, Stagecraft: The Process in VERDI

PIERLUIGI PETROBELLI

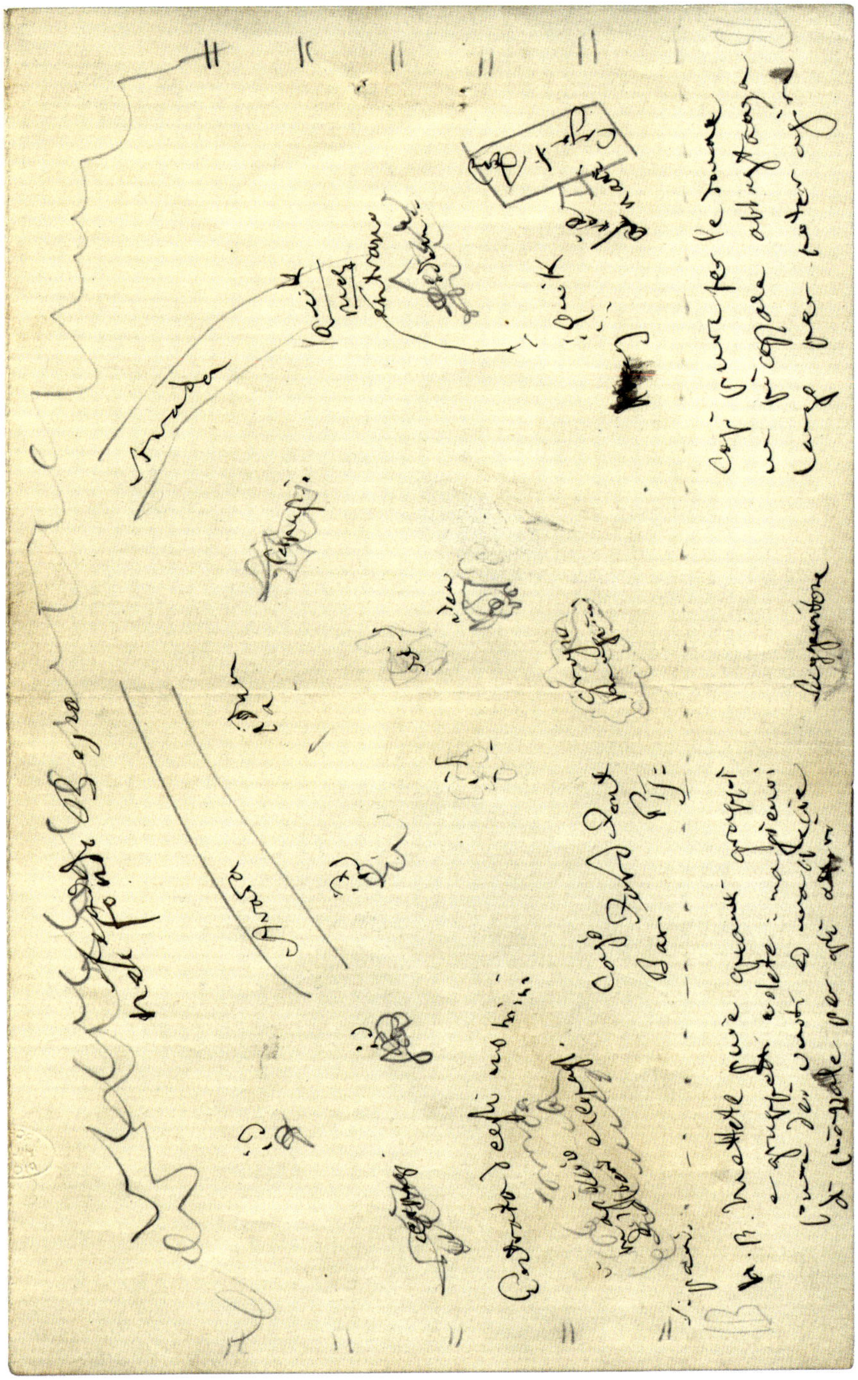

Giuseppe Verdi. Letter to Giulio Ricordi • Sant'Agata, 18 September 1892
• Verdi expresses his ideas concerning the set design for *Falstaff*

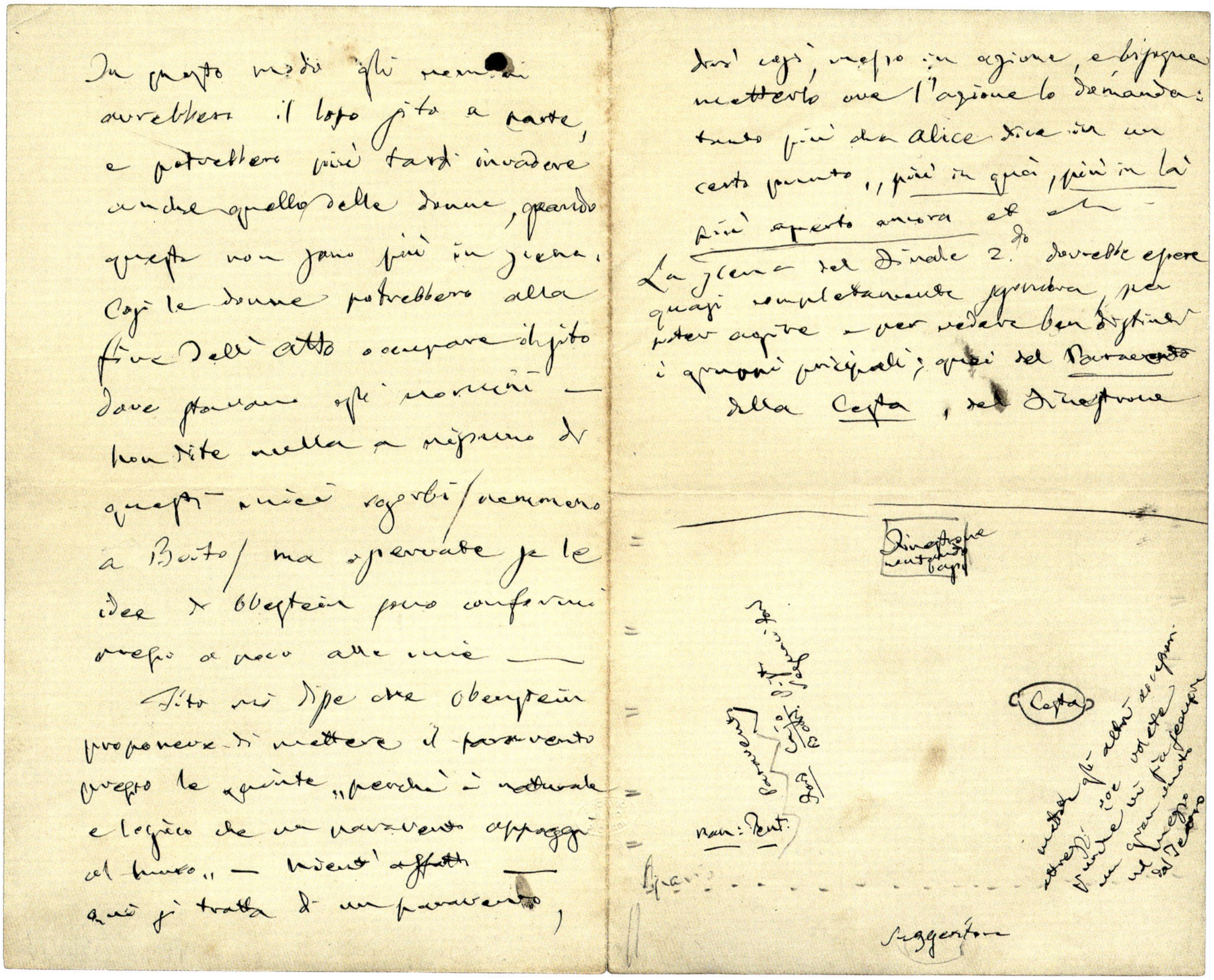
In questo modo gli uomini
avrebbero il loro sito a parte,
e potrebbero più tardi invadere
anche quello delle donne, quando
queste non sono più in scena.
Così le donne potrebbero alla
fine dell'atto occupare il sito
dove stavano gli uomini —
non dite nulla a nessuno di
questi miei scarabocchi/nemmeno
a Boito/ ma osservate se le
idee di Oberstein posson conformarsi
presso a poco alle mie —
Tito mi disse che Oberstein
proponeva di mettere il paravento
presso le quinte „perchè è naturale
e logico che un paravento appoggi
al muro„ — niente affatto —
qui si tratta di un paravento,

dirò così, messo in azione, e bisogna
metterlo ove l'azione lo domanda:
tanto più che Alice dice in un
certo punto „più in qua, più in là
più aperto ancora etc etc —
La scena del finale 2.do dovrebbe essere
quasi completamente sgombra, per
poter agire e per vedere ben distinti
i gruppi principali; quei del Paravento
della Cesta, del Finestrone

From Words to Music:
Libretto, Score, Stagecraft: The Process in VERDI

PIERLUIGI PETROBELLI

The whole second section of the first act is built around the constant onstage to-and-fro of the four wives, the four men, and the playful banter of the two lovers, Nannetta and Fenton, who temporarily leave their group to form one of their own. Each of these groups is characterized as much by the poetic text (through the type of verse employed) as by the musical language (through the meter and tempo, key, and melodic inflection chosen); their ceaseless alternation on stage perfectly captures the gradual taking shape of the trick on Falstaff, concluding with Alice's ironic quotation of his oafish profession of love that is greeted by all the wives uniting in an outburst of collective laughter. For the second scene of the second act Verdi imagined similar theatrical functions for the arrangement of the onstage elements—above all for the screen behind which Nannetta and Fenton hide to flirt. The letter to Giulio Ricordi, dated 18 September 1892, continues in this manner:

> Tito told me that Hohenstein proposes positioning the screen near the wings, because it is natural and logical that a screen should lean against a wall. By no means: this is a screen which is, as it were, put into action, and it must be placed where the action demands [...] For the 2nd finale the stage should be nearly empty so that the main groups can act and be seen distinctly: those near the screen, the basket, the large window.

Here again, the onstage vision emerges together with the dramatic discourse and its musical realization, and once more in an irresistible crescendo culminating when the basket containing Falstaff is thrown from the great open balcony at the rear of stage.

Verdi's operas have spread all over the world where they are performed today more than ever. Some of their tunes—think of such iconic examples as "La donna è mobile" from *Rigoletto*, "Va pensiero sull'ali dorate" from *Nabucco*, "La Vergine degli Angeli" from *La forza del destino*—have become emblematic of Italian music, divorced from the dramatic context for which they were conceived and in which they were placed by their author. Their overwhelming musical impact and consequent popularity stem however precisely from the utterly apposite dramatic functionality with which the composer invested them: the tune from *Rigoletto* captures the crux of the piece—a song of triumph from a dissolute rake's progress; the chorus in *Nabucco* encapsulates the hope of a social and political reality believed, at thatmoment of Italian history, to be unattainable; the air in *La forza del destino* constitutes a pause for prayer in the quest for inner peace. These are all recurring situations in human life, quite independently of the time and place in which they occur. And, to my way of thinking, it is from this that springs the deathless vitality of the melodies in which they are embodied.

Giuseppe Verdi, Letter to Giulio Ricordi • Busseto, 7 November 1870
• Verdi describes an Egyptian trumpet for the Triumphal March scene in *Aida*

1870

Lunedì

C. Giulio

Se Napoli non fosse Napoli vi direi che Mazzucato sarebbe ottimissimo per mandarlo a dirigere il D. Carlos; ma colla camorra di quel paese faressimo forse più male che bene.

Ma quale necessità vi è da riunir Direzione e Impresa per decidere se si deve dare o no l'Aida alla [illegible]? L'Impresa non basta?

Non dimenticate che la tromba in Lab. deve essere dritta

Il fa acuto forse potrà divenire crescente ma il re no.

Badate ai 12 Contrabassi, e che siano migliorati secondi violini, viole e violoncelli. Avevo dimenticato i timpani chè quelli che avete

Setting a Libretto to Music:
The Example of PUCCINI

DIETER SCHICKLING

Madama Butterfly, Giacomo Puccini
• Cover of the first edition vocal score, 1904

TRIANGOLO
con grande sentimento
(Vagamente)
rit
Mario
VIOLINO 1º
VIOLINO 2º
VIOLE
CELLI
C.BASSI
pp
mf

Setting a Libretto to Music:
The Example of PUCCINI

DIETER SCHICKLING

How does a libretto become an opera? The answer seems simple: the composer transforms the text written by the librettist into musical themes, into melodies with transitions from one theme to the other.

He fills the places without sung text, as determined by the plot, with orchestral music and thinks up one or another musical effect suggested by the libretto. But the reality is much more complicated and the extant documents on the origins of what remain Puccini's most popular operas even today, *La bohème*, *Tosca*, and *Madama Butterfly*, provide impressive proof of this.

It is well known that in the case of these works Puccini took a long time before even deciding to compose them. He discussed his plans primarily with his publisher Giulio Ricordi, whom he frequently drove to sheer desperation through his hesitation and constantly changing opinions. When Puccini finally reached the decision to compose, he by no means accepted the existing libretto straight away, but frequently continued to question not only individual passages, but even the entire structure.

A revealing example of Puccini's structural thinking going beyond the conventional logic of a libretto is provided by *La bohème*. In March 1893, just a few weeks after the première of his preceding opera *Manon Lescaut*, Luigi Illica and Giuseppe Giacosa—both of them experienced and renowned dramatists—were working on a libretto based on episodes from Henri Murger's *La Vie de bohème*, which, after extensive discussions and strong dramaturgical differences of opinion between the composer and his librettists, was more or less finished only about a year later. Among other things, an entire finished act of the libretto was deleted, namely a turbulent artists' party in the "Cortile della casa di via Labruyère N. 8," which was supposed to follow the present third act (the "Barriera"), and take place while Mimì leaves her new, but poor lover Rodolfo to turn her attentions to a young count.

Puccini was surely also disturbed by the similarity in atmosphere to the earlier scene in the Quartier Latin, and for him this meant above all the difficulty of finding suitable music. But he was probably much more disturbed by the, as it were, pedantic logic of the story narrated by the librettists. Since his earliest beginnings, Puccini the music dramatist was attracted not to the "sensible" course of a story, but rather to the stringing together of emotionally gripping situations. To this end he was prepared to accept gaps in the logic of the narrative, so that in the case of *Bohème*, due to the deletion of the Labruyère act, two different motives for Rodolfo's and Mimì's separation exist side-by-side. Puccini stubbornly maintained, against the sometimes despairing librettists, that the unity of the plot would be established by his music alone and not by an equally well-grounded logic within the

Giacomo Puccini • 1906 • With a dedication to Giulio Ricordi

al mio amato
Signor Giulio
affettuosamente
Budapest 12.IV.06
Kossák
BUDAPEST

Setting a Libretto to Music: The Example of PUCCINI

DIETER SCHICKLING

text. What Puccini aspired to, against the view of his quite skilled but more conventionally thinking librettists, was a kind of discontinuity of the dramaturgy, which is characteristic of opera's modernist awakening at the dawn of the twentieth century.

The origin of the *Tosca* libretto also manifested Puccini's crucial collaboration on the structure of his operas even before writing down a single note. Ferdinando Fontana, the librettist of his first two (rather unsuccessful) operas *Le Villi* and *Edgar*, had already in 1889 drawn his attention to the nationally and internationally successful drama of the famous French author Victorien Sardou. In accordance with Puccini's desire, the publishing house Ricordi immediately sought to acquire the rights to the work. When the publisher finally succeeded in 1891, Puccini was no longer interested, since he was in the middle of composing *Manon Lescaut*, after which *La bohème* was uppermost in his mind. Only in 1896 did he decide to compose *Tosca* after all; the libretto had been prepared years earlier by Illica, but now had to be thoroughly reworked in accordance with Puccini's ideas. This included a radical change to the ending: in the original version of Illica's libretto Tosca does not die as a result of her leap from the terrace of the Castel Sant'Angelo (as in Sardou's drama) but, in keeping with a time-honored Italian opera tradition, merely becomes insane. After discussions with Sardou (whose suggestions, incidentally, Puccini by no means accepted in full) Puccini demanded from his librettists a return to the original ending. Nor did he allow himself to be deterred by the crucial objection raised by the other librettist Giacosa: that the highly dramatic play with arguments between conflict-laden figures would lead to constant duets and left no room for the necessary solo lyricisms. By now, however, this kind of thinking within traditional schemes was long since foreign to Puccini. He composed continuous sequences with virtually no consideration to whether they gave rise to arias or duets in the classical sense—in this, he was closer to his great model Richard Wagner but also to contemporaries like Richard Strauss and Claude Debussy than to the tradition of Italian bel canto opera. It is clear that this had to lead to conflicts with the librettists, who followed conventional forms.

As in *La bohème*, in the subsequent opera *Madama Butterfly* as well there would be an extensive deletion at an advanced stage of work on the libretto. Puccini had seen the one-act drama by the American Broadway author David Belasco in June of 1900 in London and prompted Ricordi to inquire into the rights to the opera. In the spring of 1901 the librettists—once again Illica and Giacosa—set to work on a first draft, and in the summer and autumn of the same year Puccini wrote down his initial musical ideas, at times in the margins of the numerous libretto manuscripts. Only in the summer of 1902 was the libretto far enough along for the composer to state his approval. This did not prevent him from demanding the deletion of the so-called consulate act in November, after he had already begun to compose, and of making the deletion against the protestation of the librettists. Once again his reasons were of a structural and, consequently, musical nature. The visit by Pinkerton, his American wife, and Butterfly to the office of the American consul intended in the libretto would have been the only scene in the opera not to have taken place in the Japanese house purchased by Pinkerton for his sham marriage with the young geisha. The librettists thought that the change of scenery

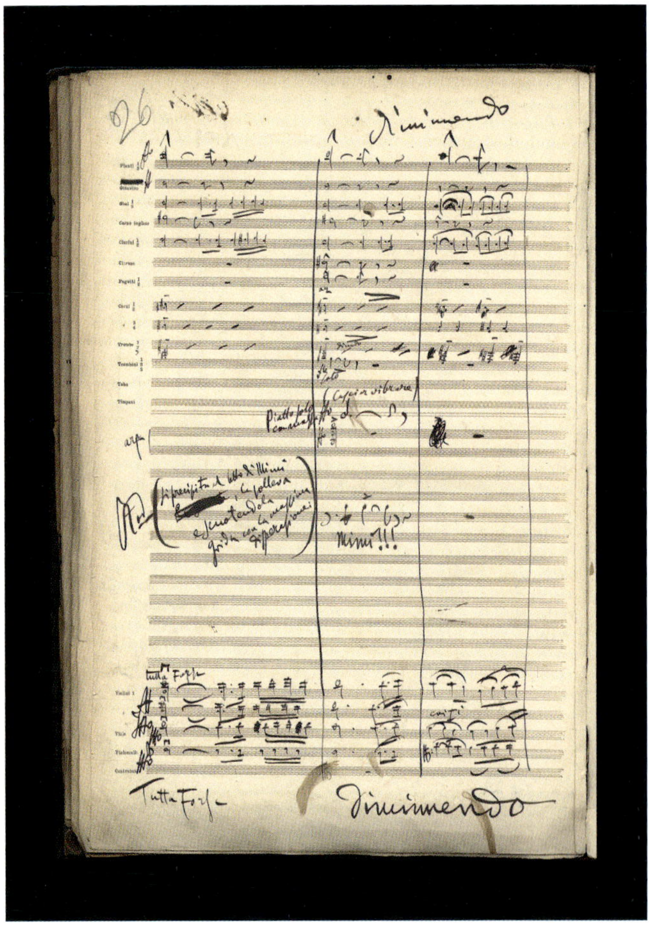

La bohème, Giacomo Puccini • Autograph score, 1896 • Mimì's death

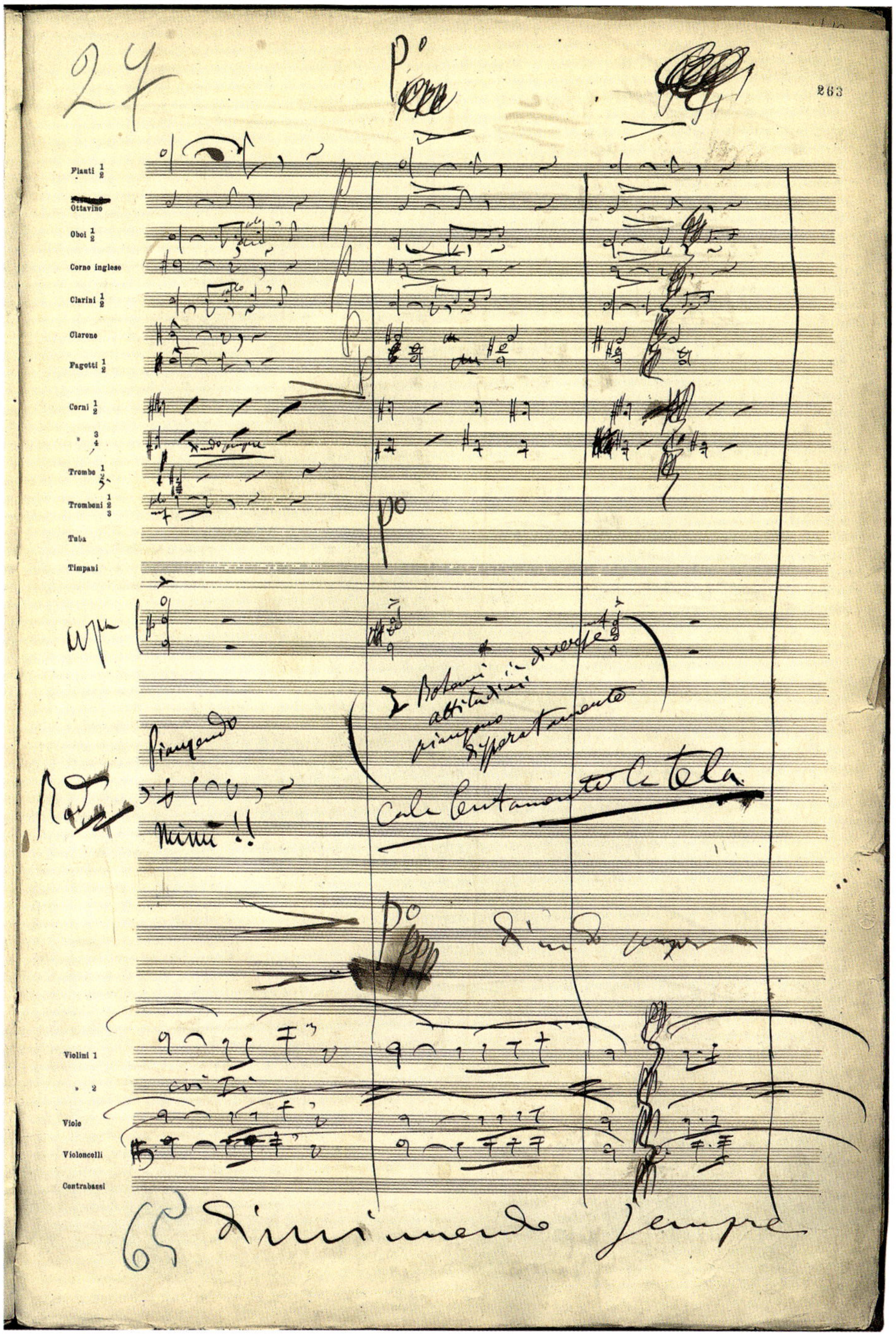
263
Flauti 1 2
Ottavino
Oboi 1 2
Corno inglese
Clarini 1 2
Clarone
Fagotti 1 2
Corni 1 2
3 4
Trombe 1 2 3
Tromboni 1 2 3
Tuba
Timpani
Piangendo
Mimì!!
Cala lentamente la tela
Violini 1
2
Viole
Violoncelli
Contrabassi
diminuendo sempre

Setting a Libretto to Music: The Example of PUCCINI

DIETER SCHICKLING

would make the juxtaposition and opposition between the American and Japanese worlds more clear. But Puccini felt that the opera had to occur continuously in a single place, in two similarly constructed and approximately equally long acts, between which lay the three years of Butterfly's wait for the return of her beloved husband. This parallelism of the two acts with beginnings and endings that were musically related to one another was more important to the composer than the change of scenery, which he rather found disturbing because it distracted from the plot's unrelenting progression towards catastrophe. He wrote to Giulio Ricordi, "As the libretto now stands it does not work after the second act, and when I noticed that I was severely troubled by it. Now, however, I have become convinced that the opera must be in two acts!! Don't let this frighten you! The Consultate [scene] was a grave error. The drama must flow to the end without interruption, quickly, effectively, frighteningly! Dividing the opera into three acts would have absolutely created a fiasco. You shall see, my dear Signor Giulio, that I am right about this." (A marginal note: It is unfortunate that after the failure of the première, Puccini retreated from this logically consistent conception under external pressure.) Significantly, this drastic change as well first occurred to him when he began composing and was unable to find appropriate music in this point of the finished libretto.

These examples clearly reveal how Puccini's compositional process began with discussions of the material and even more so of the structure of the respective libretto. At this point he apparently already had in mind a very concrete idea of what music he wanted to write and how he could write it. There are many examples of the fact that his frequent demands of the librettists to delete or fundamentally change entire passages of the text (even ones that were important to the plot) arose during his work on the music. The decisive standard for him was this: If no adequate music occurred to him, he blamed the libretto and consequently demanded that it be changed. In order to better understand this it is necessary to recall Puccini's working method, which he maintained practically unchanged throughout his life.

Puccini began with the composition of an opera by writing down sketches with varying degrees of thoroughness. These were often indications about harmonies and modulations and short rhythmic or melodic phrases, frequently accompanied by verbal remarks (for example about the key, the orchestration, or the use of motifs). Puccini generally already began with these kinds of sketches—which are not always easy to decipher—during the extremely detailed discussions with his librettists about the text. Sometimes a sheet of music contains non-continuous sketches, which shows that during sketching, Puccini was not always clear about their future role, or subsequently changed it. At a later point in time he began writing down compositional drafts, which, using the libretto, contained all the voices and, on two staffs, an instrumental accompaniment as a preliminary stage to the orchestral score, at times with verbal notes about future orchestration. These compositional drafts are not always continuous but rather each contains groupings that seemed clear to Puccini at the time. As a rule he first began with the orchestration only after an entire act had been largely completed by means of such compositional drafts. But the phases of work—sketching, compositional draft, orchestration—frequently overlap. Thus, for example, Puccini re-sketched several places during the compositional draft or corrected the draft again while he was already occupied with the orchestration.

This all took place before delivery of the manuscript score to the publishing house, which then produced from it the performance and sales materials necessary for the première (copies of the full score, choral and orchestral parts, vocal score, libretto), and this does not include the many cases (with almost all of his operas) in which Puccini made sometimes radical changes even after the première. Puccini's working method demanded constant contact with the librettists, since in the sketching phase and above all in the draft of the composition frequently the problem arose that the existing libretto text did not correspond to Puccini's musical ideas and thus new texts were necessary. But the composer, his librettists, and the publisher Giulio Ricordi, who almost always became involved, were not, as a rule, residing in the same places, but rather at quite a distance from one another—in the cases of *La bohème*, *Tosca*, and *Madama Butterfly*, for example, Puccini was in Tuscany, Illica was in Milan or Castell'Arquato near Piacenza, Giacosa was in Milan or in Colleretto in Piedmont, and Ricordi was in Milan. They therefore remained in contact by post, which at the time was astonishingly rapid. It was entirely possible for all parties involved to correspond with one another twice or three times per week.

This incomplete but fortunately largely preserved correspondence makes it possible to reconstruct the concrete work of writing the music to the librettos sometimes even in detail, including the many intermediary steps that could not always be realized. There are numerous cases in which Puccini demanded new texts from his librettists while composing, which he required for musical reasons. The following letter to

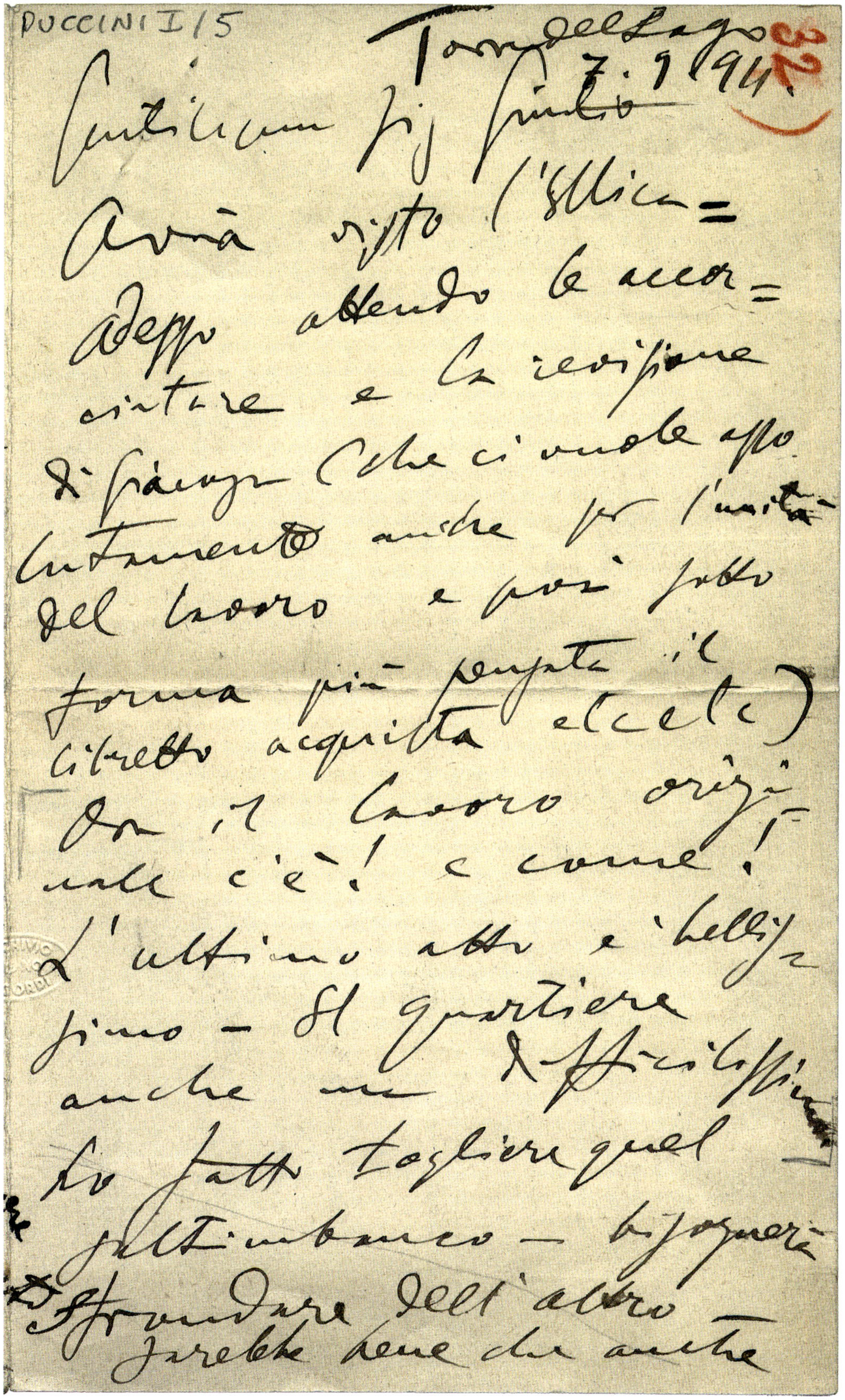
PUCCINI I/5

Torre del Lago 7.9.94

32

Gentilissimo Sig. Giulio

Avrà visto l'Illica = adesso attendo le accor = ciature e la revisione di Giacosa che ci vuole asso = lutamente anche per l'unità del lavoro e poi fatto forma più perfetta il libretto acquista etc etc) Ora il lavoro origi = nale c'è! e come! L'ultimo atto è bellis = simo – Il quartiere anche m. difficilissi = ho fatto togliere quel saltimbanco – bisognerà sfrondare dell'altro sarebbe bene che anche

Giacomo Puccini • Letter to Giulio Ricordi • Torre del Lago, 7 September 1894 • Puccini mentions he is awaiting the draft of *La bohème* from the librettists; he wants them to shorten some verses and remove unnecessary literary adornments to make the verses more suitable for his music

Setting a Libretto to Music: The Example of PUCCINI

DIETER SCHICKLING

Tosca, Giacomo Puccini • Autograph score, 1900 • "Recondita armonia"

Tosca, Giacomo Puccini • Autograph score, 1900 • "O dolci baci"

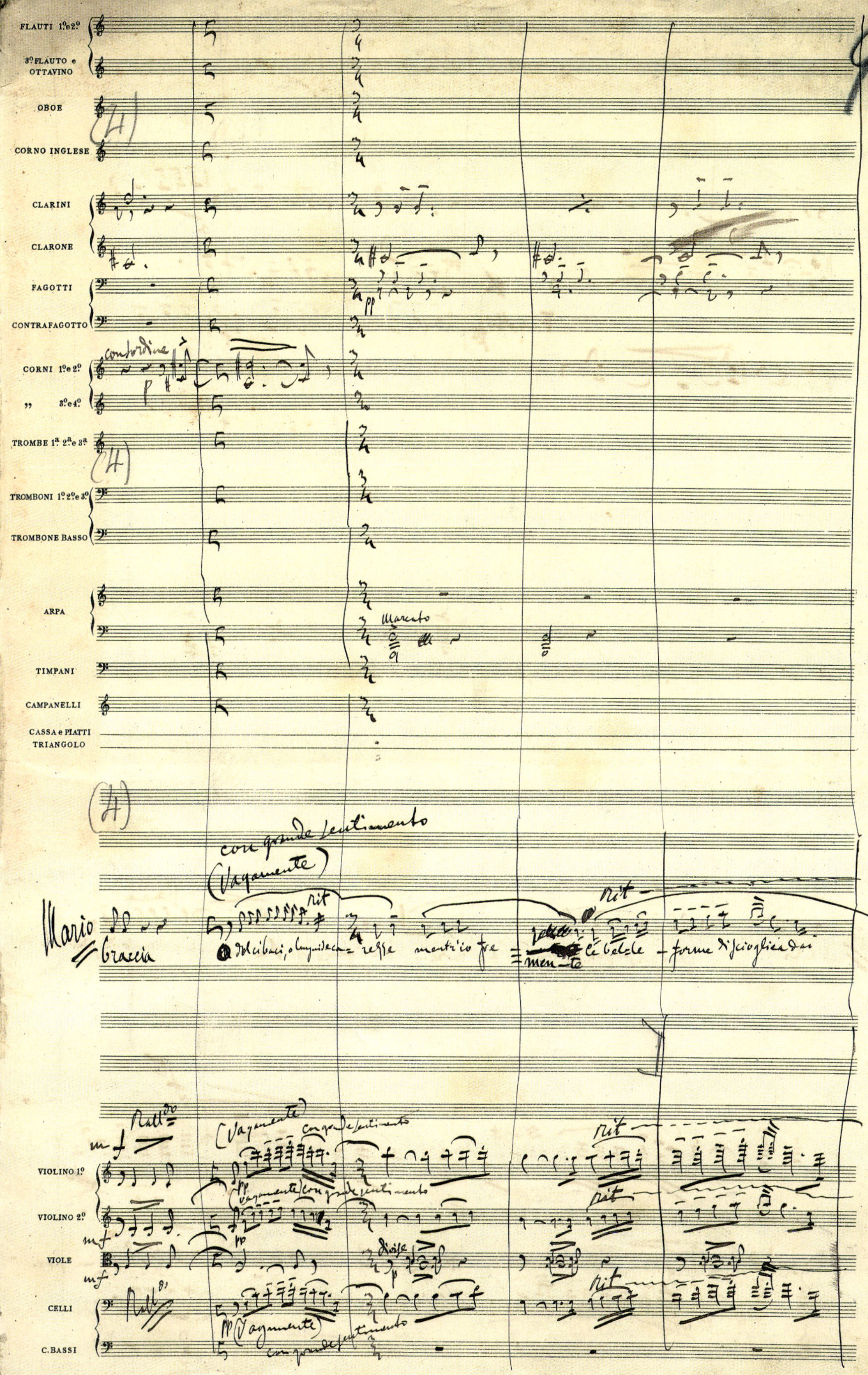
FLAUTI 1º e 2º
3º FLAUTO e OTTAVINO
OBOE
CORNO INGLESE
CLARINI
CLARONE
FAGOTTI
CONTRAFAGOTTO
CORNI 1º e 2º
„ 3º e 4º
TROMBE 1ª 2ª e 3ª
TROMBONI 1º 2º e 3º
TROMBONE BASSO
ARPA
TIMPANI
CAMPANELLI
CASSA e PIATTI
TRIANGOLO
con grande sentimento
(Vagamente)
Mario
VIOLINO 1º
VIOLINO 2º
VIOLE
CELLI
C. BASSI

Setting a Libretto to Music:
The Example of PUCCINI

DIETER SCHICKLING

Giacosa serves to demonstrate one single example, from the work on *Madama Butterfly*:

> Please send me immediately some verses for the ensemble of act 1:
>
> *dovè dovè*
> [where is he, where is he]
>
> *eccolo lì*
> [there he is]
>
> *bello non è*
> [he is not handsome]
>
> *bello è così*
> [handsome is such]
>
> *che non si può*
> [that you cannot]
>
> *sognar di più*
> [dream of anything better]
>
> etc. etc.
>
> Using this exact meter.
> Especially for the female friends and for the relatives (tenors) whom I had to insert
> Have the Uncle speak as well
> Goro can participate in the gossiping of the aunt and Butterfly. In conclusion, I need 15 or 20 of these kinds of verses, inserted among the previous ones and ending on Butterfly's line:
>
> one–two–three
> and everyone down.

The final versions of the libretto and the score at this point show that Giacosa followed the instructions here almost to the letter. In other cases, however, he did not, but rather protested loudly against the fact that in his composition Puccini was destroying the cleverly devised verse structure of the libretto, which for the poet was almost enough to damage his reputation. Behind such conflicts, that at times resulted in the published libretto text diverging from the actually composed text, stood a latent conflict at the time between composer and librettist.

Traditional Italian opera demanded a metered text in complicated rhyming verse, whose artifice (which was scarcely comprehensible even for the reader) was increasingly felt to be a burden by composers striving for ever freer forms of musical articulation. Verdi had already once dreamed of composing a prose text that would free him from the constraint of a predetermined rhythmic structure, but nonetheless never realized this dream any more than Puccini did. Puccini, at any rate, was in the end no longer concerned with the metrical scruples of his librettists but wrote his music as he felt compelled to. In this sense as well (as in many other musical respects) he disregarded the conventions of his collaborators, his time, and his country. Puccini's working method and, ultimately, that of his librettists, shows that the metamorphosis of a libretto into the music of an opera is by no means a simple process that flows, as it were, of its own accord. Rather, it is an extraordinarily complex process which, if all goes well, will in the end result in a masterpiece of music history.

Madama Butterfly, Giacomo Puccini • Autograph score, 1904
• "Un bel dì vedremo"

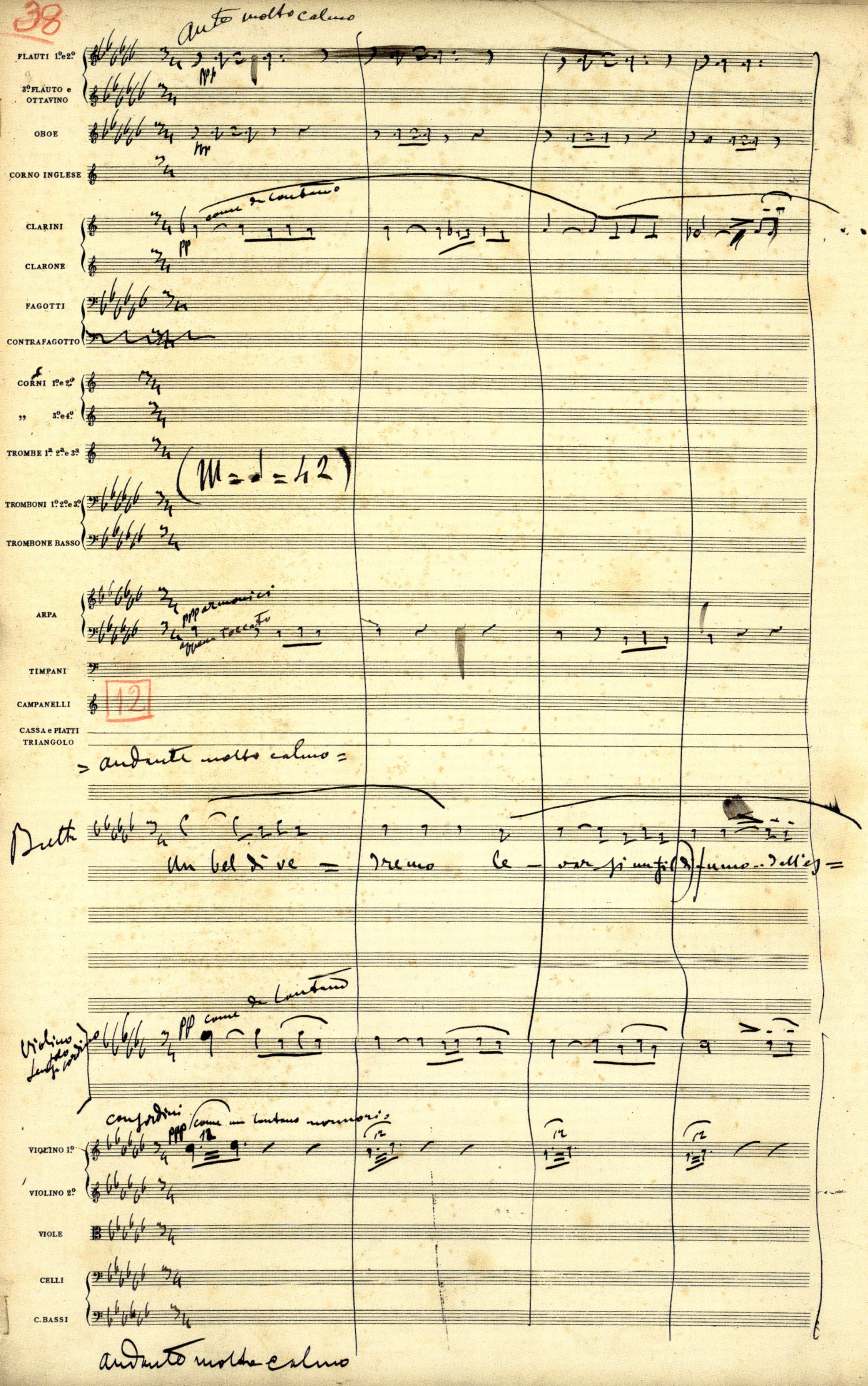
38
Ando molto calmo
FLAUTI 1º e 2º
3º FLAUTO e OTTAVINO
OBOE
CORNO INGLESE
CLARINI
come da lontano
pp
CLARONE
FAGOTTI
CONTRAFAGOTTO
CORNI 1º e 2º
„ 3º e 4º
TROMBE 1ª 2ª e 3ª
(M = ♩ = 42)
TROMBONI 1º 2º e 3º
TROMBONE BASSO
ARPA
ppp armonici
appena toccato
TIMPANI
CAMPANELLI
12
CASSA e PIATTI
TRIANGOLO
andante molto calmo =
Butt.
Un bel dì ve = dremo le = var si un fil di fumo = dall'e =
Violino senza sordino
pp come da lontano
con sordini
ppp come un lontano mormorio
12
VIOLINO 1º
VIOLINO 2º
VIOLE
CELLI
C. BASSI
andante molto calmo

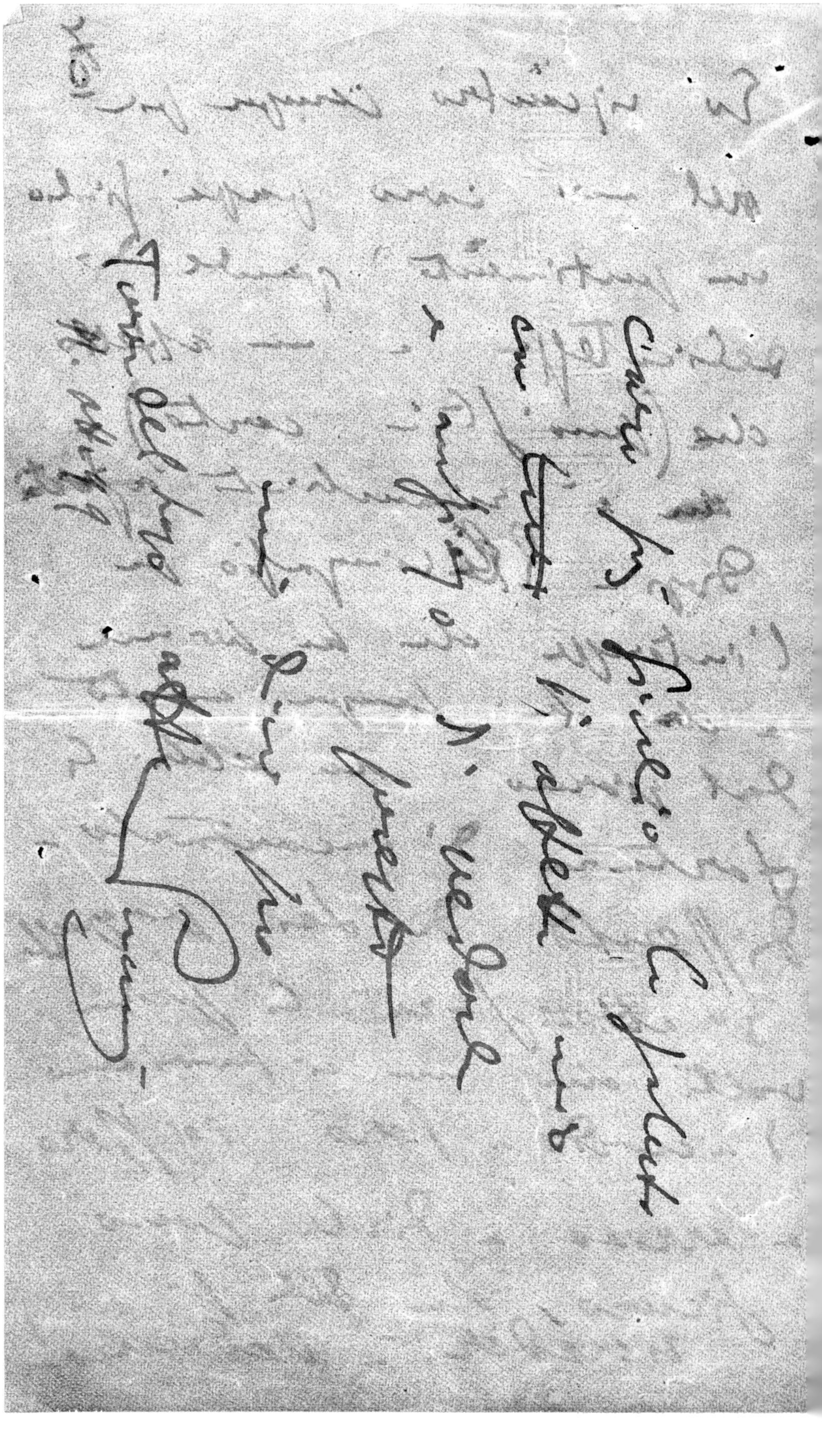
Caro Sig. Giulio La saluto
con ~~tutti~~ li affetti miei
e augurij di vederla
presto
mi dica pr
Torre del Lago aff.mo Puccini
11. ott. 99

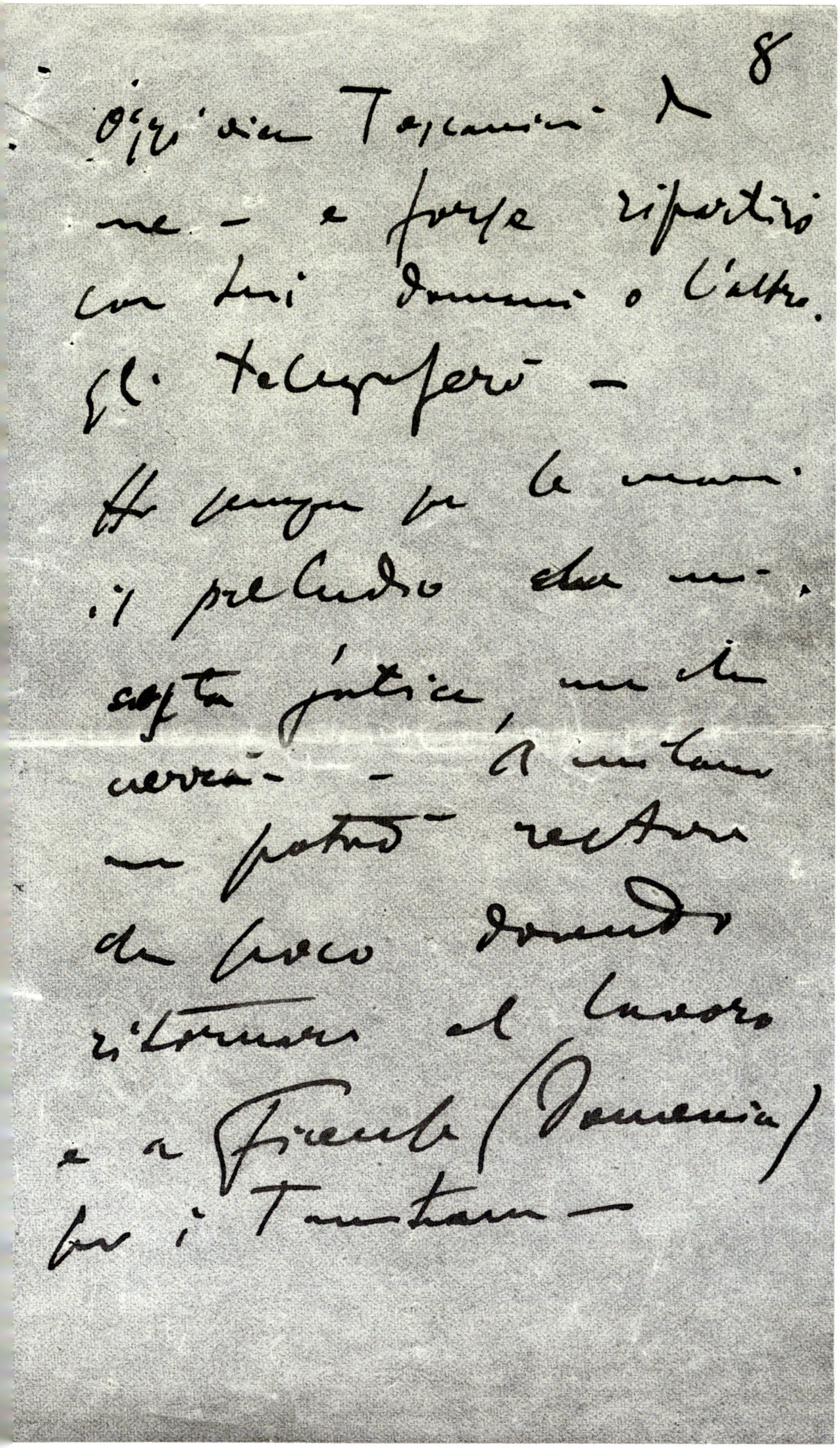
8

Oggi viene Toscanini da
me – e forse ripartirò
con lui domani o l'altro.
gli telegraferò –

Ho sempre fra le mani
il preludio che mi
costa fatica, ma che
verrà – A Milano
non potrò restare
da poco dovendo
ritornare al lavoro
e a Firenze (Domenica)
per i [illegible] –

Giacomo Puccini • Letter to Giulio Ricordi • Torre del Lago, 11 October 1899 • Puccini discusses possible changes to Act III of *Tosca* and informs Ricordi about a meeting with Arturo Toscanini.

SCENOGRAFIA

Scenography:
Perspectives on the Evolution of Operatic Staging

MERCEDES VIALE FERRERO

Madama Butterfly, Giacomo Puccini • Milan, Teatro alla Scala, 1904
• Interior of Butterfly's house, Act II • Photograph of the set design by Vittorio Rota

Scenography:
Perspectives on the Evolution of Operatic Staging

MERCEDES VIALE FERRERO

The great set designers, from Giacomo Torelli to Alessandro Sanquirico, offered their contemporaries and passed down to posterity an idealized image of their own activity: artist and quasi-sorcerer, the set designer supposedly had the ability to dominate space, transporting the audience to remote and unexplored worlds; and what was more he apparently knew how to conquer time, resurrecting the past and presaging the future.

This flattering portrait corresponded only in part with theatrical practice. In particular, in the half-century that stretched from 1853 (*Il trovatore*) to 1904 (*Madama Butterfly*) set designers did not have unlimited creative freedom and had constantly to compromise with other parties: the librettist, the composer, the music publisher.

The librettist established the *scenario* (or rather the sequence of locations in which the action was supposed to have taken place) and the set designer kept to it. Sometimes, however, the composer asked for changes to be made and in fact Puccini stepped in several times in order to impose his choices on the kinds of set designs for his operas. Luigi Illica had inserted into the plot of *La bohème* a party in a Parisian courtyard; Puccini removed it, and the courtyard disappeared from the scenario. Years later Puccini would still maintain that it had been the appropriate action to take: "Was it not on my advice that the courtyard scene was cut (and was it not the right thing to do)?"[1] Another drastic cut was that of the act in *Madama Butterfly* which Illica had set in the American Consulate in Nagasaki. With firm resolve Puccini wrote to him: "Do you know what I have discovered? That the consulate scene would have led me to a fiasco!"[2] All that remained of the corresponding set was a summary preparatory sketch.

Verdi intervened in other ways. Carlo Ferrario was the official set designer at La Scala, but when *Aida* was performed there "Verdi insisted on the involvement of the painter Magnani from Parma," as Luigi Manini, a pupil of Ferrario's, reported dryly.[3] Even if Verdi rarely acted in such an authoritarian way, during the preparations for his operas he suggested, advised, or requested specific effects and layouts for the scenes. Often he imagined them while composing. "I envisaged it when I wrote the music," he wrote concerning Ford's garden in *Falstaff*, "as nothing more than a large, authentic garden with avenues, clusters of bushes, and plants here and there."[4] His attentive eyes also focused on details that to others might have appeared petty but that to him were significant. When the censors compelled him to set the action for *La traviata* in the past, he "very reluctantly" agreed but stood his ground on one point: he "would not accept wigs."[5] In other words, he would not allow the opera to be set in the 18th century which, from the viewpoint of the Romantic era, was a time of frivolous and dissolute amours, while the love between Violetta and Alfredo was a violent, all-consuming passion.

Puccini, no less exacting and attentive, was endowed with an infallible intuition for identifying the set designer best suited to interpreting his dramatic vision; for *Il tabarro* he wanted Antonio Rovescalli[6] and he succeeded in getting him, but only a few

Aida, Giuseppe Verdi • Milan, Teatro alla Scala, 1872 • The gates of Thebes, Act II • Set design by Girolamo Magnani

SCENOGRAFIA

Scenography:
Perspectives on the Evolution of Operatic Staging

MERCEDES VIALE FERRERO

La bohème, Giacomo Puccini • Turin, Teatro Regio, 1896
• The Barrière d'Enfer, Act III • Set design by Adolf Hohenstein

La bohème, Giacomo Puccini • Paris, Opéra-Comique, 1898
• The Barrière d'Enfer, Act III • Photograph of the set design by Lucien Jusseaume

SCENOGRAFIA

Scenography:
Perspectives on the Evolution of Operatic Staging

MERCEDES VIALE FERRERO

years after the première. For *Turandot* he chose Galileo Chini,[7] but he would die without ever having seen his sets. Intolerant of the conventions that regulated the various professions in the opera houses, Puccini often turned to friends for suggestions and advice. On one occasion he wrote to a priest, Don Pietro Panichelli, for information regarding "prayers to be recited during the procession" in the first act of *Tosca* so as achieve a particular "phonic effect": "The scene is as follows: The mitered abbot, the canons etc. etc. emerge from the sacristy and proceed as the crowd gathers on both sides to watch them pass. At the front of the stage there is a character (the baritone) who soliloquizes independently—or almost—from what is going on in the background."[8] Here we see Puccini already considering elements of the staging, which shows how very tightly music and setting were, to his mind, bound up together.

Composers' interventions did not come to an end with the première of the opera. When *Aida* was revived in Parma, Verdi had the depth of the two superimposed sets in the last act reduced, but he was unsatisfied with the result and thus, for the production in Padua, he asked that the original dimensions of the Milan première be reinstated.[9] Verdi did not care for Carlo Ferrario's sets for *Otello* at La Scala (7 February 1887) because, as he wrote, "they in no way serve either the setting or the Drama";[10] thus for the performance at the Teatro Costanzi in Rome on April 18, the stage design was redone from sketches by Giovanni Zuccarelli. Starting again from scratch was, it must be said, wholly unusual in the theatrical practice of the time, when the preference was rather for keeping replicable models ("in the theater, the bad traditions are the ones that persist," noted Verdi in the letter cited above). But what were the reasons for the difficult relationship between composers and set designers? Was it a contrast of artistic tastes? Different theatrical objectives? Perhaps, more simply, there was a gap between the composer's imagination—freed as it was from practical concerns—and the imagination—governed by structural and pragmatic parameters—of the set designer, who had to visually represent the dramatic meaning while at the same time laying out the spaces and paths in which the singers, choruses, and masses interacted.

Adolf Hohenstein, the set designer who between 1893 and 1900 managed to please both Verdi for *Falstaff* and Puccini for *La bohème* and *Tosca*, was not a sorcerer but an artist capable of penetrating the plot and exploring the characters' states of mind. His name is tied to *Tosca*, for which he created two masterpieces: the poster and the set design for the scene of Castel Sant'Angelo. Each of these images, in its own particular language, communicated messages of intense emotive impact and they remain symbolic of that opera to this day. Contrary to what was then the usual practice, Hohenstein designed both the sets and the costumes, which probably contributed to the coherence of the overall production. Such coherence was all the more difficult to achieve given that Italian theaters had not yet seen the advent of the stage director or, to use Verdi's words, "a single supervisory intelligence that oversees costumes, sets, props, *mise en scène*, etc."[11]

The label of "regista" (artistic director) may be attributed to Albert Carré, director of the Opéra-Comique in Paris, for the French revival of *La bohème* (with the title *La Vie de bohème*) in 1898. This production, approved by Puccini, resurrected Paris as it was in 1830, before the complete transformation of the city that occurred during the reign of Napoleon III, and thus satisfied both the public's sense of nostalgia and the dogmatism of the critics, who demanded an exact *"couleur locale."* What was new, furthermore, was the uninhibited and lively style of acting, gestures, and movement. Puccini found the costumes designed by Marcel Multzer to be "precise" and "pretty"[12] and Lucien Jusseaume's sets to be quite imaginative and original. The sets probably owed their apparent novelty to their skillful pictorial execution since, as far as their structural layout was concerned, photographic evidence[13] reveals that Jusseaume had carefully studied the set designs of Adolf Hohenstein which had been sent to Paris by the music publisher, Giulio Ricordi.

The music publisher was perhaps the most influential interlocutor both with and for the set designer. The Ricordi publishing house (like others in Europe) hired out to theaters the scores of the operas to which it had the rights, and also owned the designs for sets, costumes, and props which it distributed as models. It was the publisher who chose and commissioned the set designer: Giulio Ricordi turned either to designers active in the theaters (such as Ugo Gheduzzi for *Manon Lescaut*, Vittorio Rota and Carlo Songa for *Madama Butterfly*) or to trusted artists (such as Adolf Hohenstein and Giuseppe Palanti). The choices of the publisher, however, did not always coincide exactly with those of the theater managers: thus it was, for instance, that the libretto for the première of *Falstaff* at La Scala credits the sets to Giovanni Zuccarelli, who had realized them but had not conceived them. Casa Ricordi's practice of circulating designs for sets and costumes was supplemented with the publication of the *disposizioni sceniche*, manuals which laid down guidelines for the entire production and which, as far as the sets were concerned, completed the prescriptive system established by circulating the designs. While the latter presented the scenes themselves, the *disposizioni* explained how to construct them, provided plans of

Madama Butterfly, Giacomo Puccini • Milan, Teatro alla Scala, 1904
• A hill near Nagasaki, Act I • Photograph of the set design by Vittorio Rota

Varischi Artico & C.o
Corso V. Em. 22
MILANO

Madama Butterfly di G. Puccini

Atto 1.º

Scenography:
Perspectives on the Evolution of Operatic Staging

MERCEDES VIALE FERRERO

their layout, listed the requisite materials, and suggested special effects and lighting techniques.

The concept of replicable stage designs had been, in a certain sense, anticipated by the founder of Casa Ricordi, Giovanni, who from 1827 to 1832 had published in fascicles the lithographs of the *Nuova raccolta di scene teatrali inventate e disegnate dal celebre Sanquirico* (New collection of theatrical sets conceived and designed by the renowned Sanquirico). These reproduced the complete sets of 34 operas and 13 ballets that had been performed in the opera houses of Milan. The aim, according to the publisher's catalog, was that they should serve as "material for study, and as a reliable guide," in other words, as exemplars.[14] The role of the music publisher in the creation of the sets acquired even greater influence with the son of Giovanni, Tito Ricordi who, at the suggestion of Verdi, published the first Italian *disposizione scenica*, that of *Giovanna de Guzman* (in actual fact a translation of Louis Palianti's *livret de mise en scène* for *Les Vêpres siciliennes*), which was followed by that of *Un ballo in maschera* complete with detailed layouts of the sets.[15] With Tito's son Giulio the system reached its greatest degree of

Madama Butterfly, Giacomo Puccini • Paris, Opéra-Comique, 1906 • A hill near Nagasaki, Act I • Set design by Marcel Jambon and Alexandre Bailly

Madama Butterfly, Giacomo Puccini • Paris, Opéra-Comique, 1906 • Interior of Butterfly's house, Act II • Set design by Marcel Jambon and Alexandre Bailly

M. Jambon et A. Bailly.

2me et 3me acte.

FALSTAFF – atto I.° – scena I.°

Falstaff, Giuseppe Verdi • Milan, Teatro alla Scala, 1893
• Interior of the Garter Inn, Act I, scene 1 • Set design by Adolf Hohenstein

SCENOGRAFIA

Scenography:
Perspectives on the Evolution of Operatic Staging

MERCEDES VIALE FERRERO

Falstaff, Giuseppe Verdi • Milan, Teatro alla Scala, 1893 • A garden: on the left, Ford's house, Act I, scene 2 • Set design by Adolf Hohenstein expansion and prescriptive rigor: in theory the set and costume designs, and the *disposizioni* represented the ideal production, to be imposed with the authority "of commercial power and of artistic power."[16] In practice, however, there was more flexibility when it came to the execution itself, since the actual conditions pertaining in the theaters necessitated modifications to the canonical models: stages varied in size, the stage machinery was not standard, and there were marked differences in available financial resources and manpower. It would be unreasonable, therefore, to define as "tyrannical" a method that had the exceptional merit of encouraging the publisher to retain such precious artistic material. Today the collection of set and costume designs preserved in the Casa Ricordi archives constitutes a veritable museum and is at the same time an indispensable resource for understanding the history of operatic staging between 1848 and 1936, allowing us to study it at the planning stages, as "work in progress."

The systematic documentation of the sets and *mises en scène* established by Casa Ricordi also makes it possible to observe a curious paradox: the more detailed the instructions were, the more quickly they became outdated, a consequence of subsequent technical innovations. The music critic Filippo Filippi, reviewing the première of *Aida* in Cairo observed: "The last scene of the underground vault with the temple above remains a problem [...] because, instead of the light being evenly distributed, the subterranean room should be dark like a cellar, and the temple above should be blazing with light, possibly electric."[17] In 1871-72 electric light was produced by heavy, cumbersome Voltaic arc "machines," which few theaters owned; indeed in the *disposizione* for *Aida* Giulio Ricordi continued to specify "lighting devices, which ideally will be gas-powered" for the temple (p. 63). A decade later, in 1884, La Scala would be equipped with an Edison electrical system, rendering gas lighting obsolete.

Among the new technologies with possibilities for theatrical use, photography was widely exploited as a means of authenticating the locations represented. Giulio Ricordi did not fail to inform the public that for the première of *Madama Butterfly* at La Scala (17 February 1904) "the harbor and the city of Nagasaki were copied from a large colored photograph and similarly the interior of Butterfly's little house, its dimensions only having to be suitably enlarged to fit the requirements of the stage."[18] To his mind the creation of an "authentic" image was, therefore, a significant feature. The Casa Ricordi archives possess two photographs of Nagasaki: the panorama of the port and the view of a canal lined with small houses. Vittorio Rota's set for the first act is a "collage" of these two sources: on the right the backdrop depicts "the harbor and the city," while the house is in the foreground on the left, connected to the background by a garden Rota imagined without a specific model. The effect is fragmentary, uneven, especially in the enlarged dimensions of the full-size set. For the interior of the little house in the second act the set designer, Carlo Songa, also made use of photographs, "authentic" in their own way because they documented a stage production of David Belasco's play *Madame Butterfly*; in other words a Japan "made in the USA" and then scaled up to the dimensions of La Scala's vast stage. Cio-Cio-San's house seemed like "a kind of Buddhist temple" to Albert Carré, who had seen *Butterfly* in London and decided that for the Opéra-Comique in Paris another arrangement was necessary. The new set designs, commissioned from Marcel Jambon and Alexandre Bailly, can be found in the Ricordi archives thanks once again to the intervention of Puccini who, "declaring never to have seen anywhere a comparable production of his work, had the sets redone in all the theaters as soon as he got back to Italy."[19]

What was the difference between the two productions? It was not one of method, since Carré too had sought *"couleur locale"* and had collected a series of publications, objects, and documents as sources. But Carré's choices were different, favoring instead a series of images for their symbolic function. Puccini understood the importance of these images and described them in a letter to Giulio Ricordi.[20] In the first act the *torii* (open gateway) and the footbridge are characteristic elements of the Japanese landscape: but the *torii* also denotes the presence of a temple, and therefore sets up the arrival of the bonze, Butterfly's uncle, "to excellent effect" while the bridge symbolizes passage. In crossing it, Butterfly passes (with no possibility of return) from one shore to the other, from one people to another, from the "time of playful youth" to the "call of love." In the second act the typical raised structure of the little house, with "its own small set of footlights," almost a theater within a theater, isolated Butterfly in her solitary "persistent vigil." Carré then surrounded her with an array of "authentic" objects that not only paid tribute to the fashion for *japonisme* but also served to illustrate the protagonist's state of mind. Cio-Cio-San thus emerges from her butterfly cocoon, blinded by the "American dream," to be seen as the creature of an ancient civilization, of a refined cultural world that she had abandoned for love but from which she would, in her final moments, draw the dignity of dying "with honor." Giulio Ricordi, at first skeptical about Carré's innovations,[21] ended up accepting them; indeed he published the Parisian *livret de mise en scène*[22] and distributed it to theaters, as is proved by the existence of a copy in Vienna.[23]

FALSTAFF - atto 1° - scena 2°

Falstaff, Giuseppe Verdi • Milan, Teatro alla Scala, 1893
• A room in Ford's house, Act II, scene 2 • Set design by Adolf Hohenstein

SCENOGRAFIA

Scenography:
Perspectives on the Evolution of Operatic Staging

MERCEDES VIALE FERRERO

The belief that there was an optimal and normative staging did not therefore mean that the model could not be modified or indeed substituted altogether. In any case deciding how to stage an opera was the result of a network of the various sources of input—a process that is very evident in the genesis of the scenography for Verdi's *Falstaff*. The original scenario by Arrigo Boito and approved by Verdi envisaged the following:

Act I 1. Interior of the Garter Inn [...] Door in the background, door on the left
2. Garden. On the left Ford's house. Clusters of trees in the center of the stage

Act II 3. Interior of the Garter Inn as in the First Act
4. A hall in Ford's house. Large window in the background. Door on the right, door on the left

Act III 5. A village square. On the right, the outside of the Garter Inn
6. Windsor Park. In the center, Herne's great oak tree

There were therefore two sets per act, alternately "short" and "long" (depending on their depth). An equal number of internal and external scenes were distributed in a fairly traditional pattern: internal-external/ internal-internal/ external-external. In his letters to Arrigo Boito and to Giulio Ricordi, Verdi was most insistent that the staging be kept simple: "Nothing other than a large, realistic garden"; "You speak of sets, of sending painters to London (to do what?)"; "And, for the love of God, let's not do as was done for *Otello* where, in a bid to do things too well, it ended up being overdone"; "In terms of stage mechanism there is little to do, apart from the scene of the large laundry basket, which even so should not be at all difficult provided that one does not make things unnecessarily complicated"; "a *mise en scène* without particular demands (and it's better that way)."[24] Thus wrote Verdi, although he did have certain "demands" because he sent Giulio Ricordi various sketches for the garden and the hall (which Pierluigi Petrobelli discusses elsewhere in this volume: see pp. 67). Fearing that the set designs might not convey an adequate impression of the scenes, Verdi noted: "Some *maquettes* [scale models] need to be made so that we are in a position, should it be necessary, to work out solutions once we're at the rehearsal stage."[25] In fact Hohenstein produced a series of *maquettes* "with all the 'flats' and the 'practicables' in place," which made it possible to "view and evaluate in minute detail every aspect of the set."[26]

These scale models for *Falstaff* have not survived, but the Casa Ricordi archives do preserve three large layouts of the sets printed in various colors, one for each act (therefore each sheet refers to the layouts of two scenes). In the lower margin of the plans is a scale intended for use with a 22-meter-wide stage, but adaptable to any other by means of simple proportion adjustments. There are also detailed printed instructions for various staging elements, whether they be props, furniture, equipment, or even what stage tricks to use. An exact correspondence can be observed between Hohenstein's designs and these plans, which also incorporate many requests made by Verdi during the mounting of *Falstaff*. Color printing makes it easier to understand the structure of the sets and how set changes were achieved, with the constituent elements of the first scene of each act being marked in red and those of the second scene in green. It is thus possible to see that the scene changes "in full view" of the public were very limited: the interior of the Inn has a depth, from the front curtain to the backdrop, of barely four meters and, to make it disappear, the stagehands had only to withdraw two wing flats and raise a backdrop with two drop scenes. It was also necessary to remove the table and the big chair, whilst an isolated bush moves into view. Behind the Inn the garden had been ready for some time, with three full flats of trees and five partial flats of "clusters of bushes here and there," as Verdi had requested. Ford's house, much further to the rear, is a three-dimensional, "parapeted" structure.

The interval between the first and second acts provided an opportunity to dismantle the garden and install the hall in Ford's house that at the start remained hidden by the backdrop and the drop scene of the Inn; between these, invisible to the public, was the large basket in which Falstaff would have to hide. Following Verdi's advice, "unnecessary complications" were avoided and the traditional trick of the trap door was used. Falstaff could thus calmly descend into the understage area while the bottomless—but supposedly full—basket ("It's heavy!" "Come on!" "The bottom went *crack*!") was carried onto the stage and lowered into a special pit hidden by a functional platform 20 cm high. There was some discussion about the props: Hohenstein thought it "natural and logical that a screen should lean against the wall," while Verdi maintained that it should be placed "where the action demands it."[27] As a consequence, the screen is not mentioned among the various furnishings and items of furniture (fireplace, curtains, blanket chest, wardrobe) that lined the walls of the hall.

Falstaff, Giuseppe Verdi • Milan, Teatro alla Scala, 1893
• Herne's Oak in Windsor Park, Act III, scene 2 • Set design by Adolf Hohenstein

FALSTAFF - atto III - scena II.
Hohenstein

Scenography:
Perspectives on the Evolution of Operatic Staging

MERCEDES VIALE FERRERO

The next set change took place during the second interval and, at the opening of the third act, Windsor Park was ready behind the square, which was of much reduced depth and was made to disappear by removing a wing flat and a side cloth (*teletta*) on each side and raising the backdrop. At the very front of the stage there advanced "in full view" a "padded platform": this prop would be a mystery if a note written by Verdi did not clarify the matter for us: "In this scene Falstaff remains lying on the ground in an uncomfortable position for more than five minutes! It might be problematic! Nevertheless let's leave things as they are for now, but we need to think ahead."[28] The problem was solved by padding out the platform on which the roots of Herne's Oak were painted; these roots are visible, protruding and entangled, in Hohenstein's design. Lights on the stage (marked on the layout as "banks of lamps") were concealed by the practicable intended for the "Entrance of the Spirits." These lights in the final nighttime scene owe their presence to Verdi, who in two letters requested "for the Park scene [...] *a shadow of darkness* that allows the audience to see the artists' faces" and "a bit of light during Garbin's *Sonnet*" (Edoardo Garbin sang the role of Fenton).[29]

In conclusion, the (relative) simplicity Verdi sought for the staging of *Falstaff* was the fruit of an attentive study of every detail and of thorough preparation, as evidenced both by his correspondence and by the equally precise and meticulous plans that are preserved in the Casa Ricordi archives. Were these plans circulated in the theaters? Can they be linked to a (perhaps lost) production manual? Such possibilities cannot be ruled out, particularly since productions of *Falstaff* in subsequent years were staged in similar fashion.

Alfred Roller and Anton Brioschi's set designs for Gustav Mahler's production of *Falstaff* at Vienna's Hofoper on 3 May

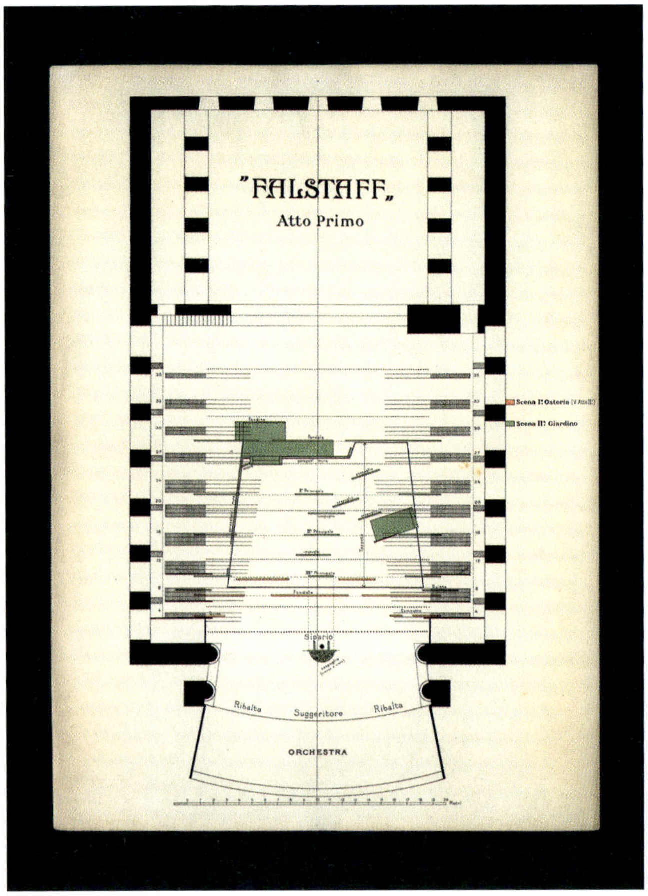

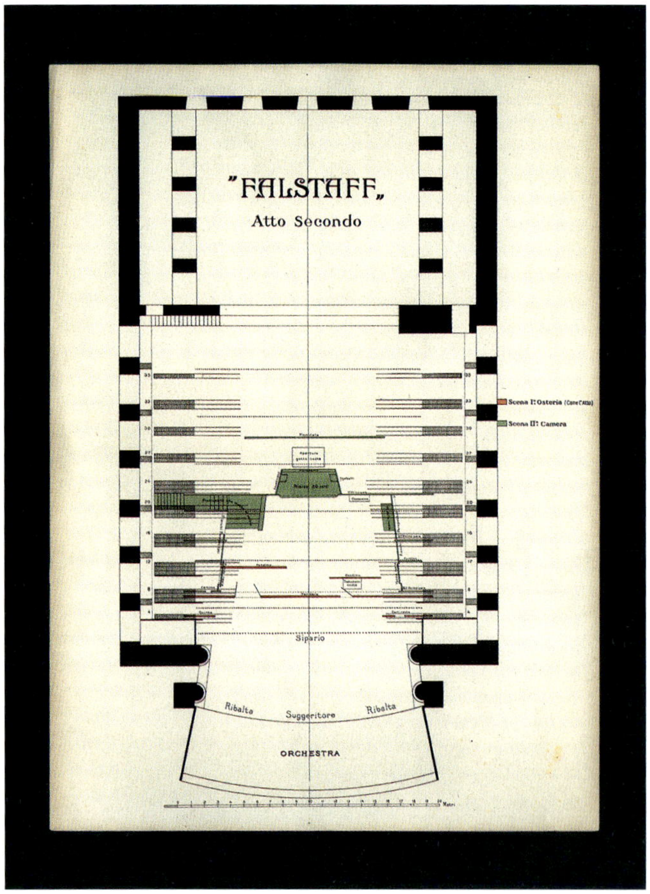

Falstaff, Giuseppe Verdi • Milan, Teatro alla Scala, 1893 • Stage plan for the two scenes in Act I

Falstaff, Giuseppe Verdi • Milan, Teatro alla Scala, 1893 • Stage plan for the two scenes in Act II

Falstaff, Giuseppe Verdi • Milan, Teatro alla Scala, 1893 • Stage plan for the two scenes in Act III

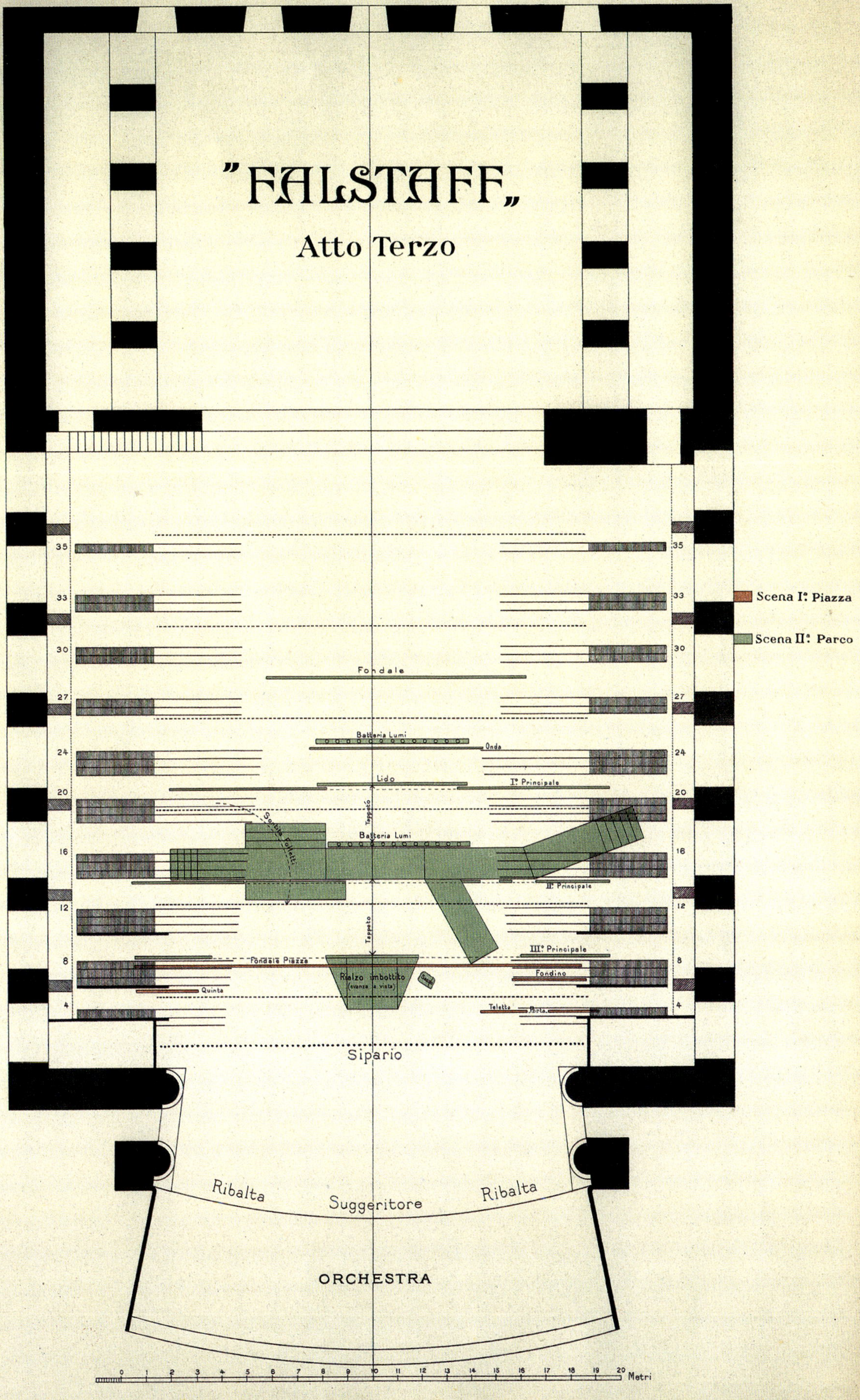

"FALSTAFF"
Atto Terzo
Scena I.ª Piazza
Scena II.ª Parco
Fondale
Batteria Lumi
Onda
Lido
I.º Principale
Tappeto
Batteria Lumi
II.º Principale
III.º Principale
Fondale Piazza
Rialzo imbottito
(avanza a vista)
Fondino
Quinta
Teletta
Porta
Sipario
Ribalta
Suggeritore
Ribalta
ORCHESTRA
Metri

Scenography:
Perspectives on the Evolution of Operatic Staging

MERCEDES VIALE FERRERO

1904 reflect the taste of the Viennese Secession and consequently seem at first sight very different from Hohenstein's. The structural and spatial arrangement, however, remained unaltered: the doors of the Inn, the garden wall, Ford's house, the furnishings of the hall (staircase, fireplace, large window, wardrobe, curtains), and the area of the trap door are still in the same positions. But there is a single, ingenious variant: growing in the square is an ancient oak tree that at night will become Herne's Oak.[30] In the revivals of *Falstaff* at La Scala in 1913, with sets by Angelo Parravicini, and in 1942-43, with sets by Mario Vellani Marchi, the garden and the hall were altered considerably in terms of their appearance, but actually very little in terms of their spatial structures: there were more or less bushes, vases of flowers, benches in the garden, the fireplace was more or less big, the stairs in the hall more or less steep, but Ford's house was always on the left, the laundry basket always toward the right, the large window always at the back.[31] What could be defined as "Verdian" stage design was therefore functional, even if other solutions have also been effective and valid, when realized by set designers "who are not so vain as to assert their own skill but who serve the Drama," [32] to borrow the phrase written by Verdi to Giulio Ricordi during preparations for *Falstaff*.

Giacomo Puccini. Letter to Giulio Ricordi • Paris, 13 January 1899
• Puccini refers to an encounter with Victorien Sardou and their discussions concerning the set design for *Tosca*

bel tipo, tutto vita, pieno
e pieno di inesattezze storiche
Topo-panoramiche -
La reprise dunque fu
buonissima - vero entusiasmo,
il 3° con relativo
bis di tutto il quartetto
un bis domandato a
grandi grida cosa strana
e non mai veduta
qui - Oggi più di

VOCI E COSTUMI

The Good, the Bad, and the Ugly:
Character and Costume in the Theater of VERDI and PUCCINI

VITTORIA CRESPI MORBIO

Madama Butterfly, Giacomo Puccini • Milan, Teatro alla Scala, 1904
• Studies of kimonos by Giuseppe Palanti

The Good, the Bad, and the Ugly:
Character and Costume in the Theater of VERDI and PUCCINI

VITTORIA CRESPI MORBIO

In 1880, Casa Ricordi's young costumier Alfredo Edel (1856-1912) was coming to grips with the new production of Giuseppe Verdi's Rigoletto. *Against all expectations, there issued from his brush a slender, graceful figure, bowing submissively like a servant in order to conceal his physical deformity. Where Verdi had boldly and proudly presented a hunchback in the theater, thirty years later Edel transformed Rigoletto to normality, as if to expunge the ignominy of his ugliness.*

It could hardly have been otherwise: Edel was a representative of that *joie de vivre* which, beginning in the second half of the 19th century, was to delight emergent bourgeois audiences in theaters and music-halls. He was the best-known Italian costumier of the age. In step with the present, he reflected the latest tastes and trends and even anticipated new models to come. His designs for costumes were much admired by music critics who noted their originality, good taste, and exquisite elegance. Ladies would pick up details in the elaborate accessories and up-to-date refinements in make-up, while gentlemen were entranced by the eye-popping short hemlines of the ballerinas which contributed to the triumph of fashionable ballets at Milan's Teatro alla Scala such as *Excelsior* (1881), *Amor* (1886), and *Sport* (1897).

In Verdi's eyes Edel seemed an eternal youth ever ready to toast Bacchus, a dandy who charmed the ladies, an eccentric man-about-town who impishly approached an art that was all froth, equally sensitive to the grace of a ribbon, to a hat with bizarre feathers, or to a daring neckline. Nevertheless the costumier, who doubtless preferred the ballets of choreographer Luigi Manzotti to the more austere demands of Verdi's dramas, was won over by the grand old man and quietly placed his talents in the service of *Otello* (Teatro alla Scala, 1887). At the apex of his career, Edel thus found himself faced with an opera not of effect but of acute psychology. In giving a face to figures such as Jago and Otello, the artist abandoned his predilection for an effervescent aesthetic of ideal beauty and plumbed instead the human mind, endowing the labyrinthine malevolence of Jago and the morbid jealousy of Otello with a tangible presence, a color, a shape, even a gait.

In composing the piece, Verdi had tried to "see," to visualize his characters, before waiting in vain for the appearance of the "Jago with the look of a man of honor"[1] he had been promised by the painter Domenico Morelli. Once the music was finished, the composer could at last describe the human undercurrent of Jago's seething envy to his costumier. The première featured Victor Maurel as Jago, clean-shaven the better to project the ambiguous, mean-spirited expression of Otello's ensign. By a kind of luciferous alchemy, the dark cloth he wears, "black, as black as his soul,"[2] is furnished with a red lining. Maurel's zestful physique, icy gaze, and imposing attitude all suggest a fascinating, magnetic presence.

Over the years, Verdi's theatrical awareness had reached full maturity, so that he would follow every aspect of the performance, even, and unusually for the time, suggesting ideas about stage direction. In the composer's eyes, staging had acquired

Madama Butterfly, Giacomo Puccini • Milan, Teatro alla Scala, 1904 Croquis Japonais. Tokyo, 1886 • Booklet with impressions of Japanese life used as a guideline by the costume and the set designers

CROQUIS JAPONAIS
PAR
G. Bigot.
1886.
TOKIO

The Good, the Bad, and the Ugly:
Character and Costume in the Theater of VERDI and PUCCINI

VITTORIA CRESPI MORBIO

Rigoletto, Giuseppe Verdi • Milan, Teatro alla Scala, 1880
• Rigoletto, Acts I and III • Costume design by Alfredo Edel

Otello, Giuseppe Verdi • Milan, Teatro alla Scala, 1887
• Otello, Act I • Costume design by Alfredo Edel

The Good, the Bad, and the Ugly:
Character and Costume in the Theater of VERDI and PUCCINI

VITTORIA CRESPI MORBIO

Otello, Giuseppe Verdi • Milan, Teatro alla Scala, 1887
• Jago, Act I • Costume design by Alfredo Edel

Falstaff, Giuseppe Verdi • Milan, Teatro alla Scala, 1893
• Falstaff, Act III • Costume design by Adolf Hohenstein

VOCI E COSTUMI

The Good, the Bad, and the Ugly: Character and Costume in the Theater of VERDI and PUCCINI

VITTORIA CRESPI MORBIO

fundamental importance: the designer's task was not only to devise a costume, but also to come up with a complete character; in his turn, the actor had to know how to wear the costume and get under the skin of the role so as to appear believable. The composer thus demanded clarity and focus, with few distractions: he was impatient with Casa Ricordi's skillfully managed publicity campaign for the world première of *Otello* and thought superfluous Edel's proposed trip to Venice to undertake a rigorous scholarly study of 16th-century arms and armor in the paintings of Vittore Carpaccio and Gentile Bellini. The head of the firm, Giulio Ricordi, who had commissioned the new opera, was well aware of the demands of the public and critics, who both gauged the quality of a piece on the historical accuracy of the production. Verdi thought otherwise, striving to discover ways to depict the metamorphosis of Otello, a victorious *condottiero* who falls prey to darker impulses.

In Edel's sketches the Moor of Venice gradually throws off the trappings of the Hammer of the Turks, dressing more and more simply in an outward sign, as it were, of his wounded pride. In recent years, Mario Del Monaco's Otello is unsurpassed, though limited to the single dimension of the victorious general who upon his entrance lets fly a triumphant *Esultate!* "with a voice that is warm, manly, robust."[3] On the other hand, film director Franco Zeffirelli took advantage of his experience in the movies to guide Placido Domingo towards the character's more deeply introspective regions. For the production at La Scala of 1976, the Spanish tenor turned to Cinecittà's make-up man, Otello Fava, who fitted him with a short wig to give further prominence to the protagonist's ample if vulnerable physique. In 1887, Edel had shown his ability at conjuring up male faces, but had no success with an identity for Desdemona, an angelic presence, pure in heart. In the sketches, Otello's unfortunate consort appears modeled on the prototype of the generalized fictional heroine. In the intimacy of the bridal chamber, her recherché apparel and impeccable coiffure and make-up appear as if, in the murder scene, the costumier was trying to allow her to make an exit with her dignity intact.

For *Falstaff* (Teatro alla Scala, 1893) Verdi could instead count on the assistance of the like-minded Adolf Hohenstein (1854-1928), a tireless, rigorous autodidact with an extraordinary instinct for the theater who forged a profound friendship with Verdi. His costume designs for Verdi's final opera seem to flow from the pen with ease, steadily, and following an organic conception of the drama. The protagonist, with all his weaknesses, is presented as a true "character" and not as the grotesque mask adopted by many future baritones.[4] The authoritarian conductor Arturo Toscanini, a cellist in the La Scala orchestra at the time Verdi was working on *Otello* and an advocate of the composer's rigorous approach to theater production, recalled that Falstaff should be neither jolly nor coarse: "He is not a comic character [*buffo*] as he is thought to be and as he is conceived and performed by so many artists."[5] In Hohenstein's drawings, Falstaff is represented as if he moves on stage with a natural vitality that would be quite alien to Edel's figures. *Falstaff*'s costumier not only heeded Verdi's suggestions, but also engaged with his protagonist's more human aspects, from waiting in trepidation for a tryst to throwing himself wholeheartedly into the identity-swapping games of the last act.

Revealing of their creator's self-absorption, Edel's nervous figures dart away, showing off matching color schemes and perfectly cut attire: the women, cutthroats, and knaves alike glide over the paper as if on the catwalk. *Falstaff*'s simplicity was better suited to winning Verdi's approbation. In Hohenstein's world there is a sense of solidity, of concreteness, as well as of compassion, that was well attuned to the sensibility of a Puccini, all of whose premières the costumier was to oversee up until *Madama Butterfly*. The artist was omnipresent as *Falstaff* advanced, instinctively aware that he was involved in the one and only opera he was to work on with the maestro. In England, he followed in Shakespeare's footsteps, taking inspiration from Sir John Gilbert's compositions for the masquerade scene. In Milan, he depicted the composer in a room in which the singers are rehearsing at the piano, on a chair, legs crossed, capturing the restrained simplicity of the aged composer; he also showed him, seen from the back, in the stage manager's room. Then the figure of Verdi seems to fade, remaining out of sight until 1901, when, on his deathbed, the great musician is portrayed in his last throes. Hohenstein's drawings of a master musician—who was almost a father figure to him—as he is gradually overtaken by death were to accompany the artist's every step; in a few years Hohenstein would leave Italy for Germany, and would look back on his Italian years fondly for the rest of his life.

Born in St. Petersburg to German parents and growing up in Vienna, Hohenstein's theatrical baptism occurred in 1884 with an opera by Puccini, *Le Villi* (Teatro Dal Verme, Milan), followed by *Edgar* (Teatro alla Scala, 1889), *Manon Lescaut* (Teatro Regio, Turin, 1893) and, after an excursion into Verdi for *Falstaff*, *La bohème* (Teatro Regio, Turin, 1896). Only four years older than Puccini, Hohenstein's artistic maturity overlapped with that of the composer, as he undertook the complementary roles of set-designer, costumier, and poster-artist, eventually acquiring the prestigious position of art director in Casa Ricordi.

La bohème, Giacomo Puccini • Turin, Teatro Regio, 1896 • Mimì with candle, Act I • Costume design by Adolf Hohenstein

The Good, the Bad, and the Ugly:
Character and Costume in the Theater of VERDI and PUCCINI

VITTORIA CRESPI MORBIO

Tosca, Giacomo Puccini • Rome, Teatro Costanzi, 1900
• Tosca, Act I • Costume design by Adolf Hohenstein

Tosca, Giacomo Puccini • Rome, Teatro Costanzi, 1900
• Scarpia, Acts I and II • Costume design by Adolf Hohenstein

Madama Butterfly, Giacomo Puccini • Milan, Teatro alla Scala, 1904 • Cio-Cio-San wearing a blue kimono, Act I • Costume design by Giuseppe Palanti

Madama Butterfly, Giacomo Puccini • Milan, Teatro alla Scala, 1904
• Chorister, Act I • Costume design by Giuseppe Palanti

The Good, the Bad, and the Ugly:
Character and Costume in the Theater of VERDI and PUCCINI

VITTORIA CRESPI MORBIO

Puccini was to trust this almost over-committed but solid and confident painter who showed such patient understanding of the composer's uneasy spirit in its ceaseless quest for certainty. Hohenstein is a familiar presence with an eloquent brush that infuses the paper with just the kind of atmosphere Puccini liked most. In place of the well-defined characters Verdi called for, here we have thumbnail sketches presenting extraordinary frescoes of Christmas revelers as they gather in the Latin Quarter for *La bohème*, or prelates, Swiss guards, and a cortege for the solemn liturgy of *Tosca*. Full of a bustling, humane poetry, likenesses of Puccini and his librettists, Illica and Giacosa, playfully peep out from among numerous little figures drawn for characters in *La bohème*.

The words the composer used to define his own musical world can be applied to Hohenstein's universe: "poetry," "simplicity," "emotion," "human vibrancy." Both are artists who smile at life—at peddlers and urchins, at lasses doing their darning, at priests and constables: slices of everyday life that are moving testimonies of an age not so long past. Hohenstein's costumes do not possess the dazzling inventiveness of those of Edel, who could wave a magic wand and transmogrify a piece of cloth into a garment of pure imagination. This was because the German artist adhered more to historical evidence and documentary truth so as to conjure up dozens of different figures with the power of conciseness. Even before going on stage, the meaning of Puccini's opera is already conveyed on paper in all its intensity: every design for *La bohème* evinces an almost tactile sense of empathy, from the cold that grips the little team of street-sweepers to Musetta's vain ingenuousness to Mimì's defenseless fragility. Life courses through this spirited, motley crew, while Mimì's fated youth seems symbolized by a candle-end gutted by a single stroke that leaves the theater in total blackness.[6]

For the artist, working with Puccini meant he had to immerse himself emotionally in a dense universe of seemingly insignificant things: every experience represented not only a new creative departure, but an effort to touch the heart strings and breathe life into figures whose sartorial style veers from severe Napoleonic (*Tosca*) to Louis Philippe (*La bohème*). The artist rapidly sketched his characters on paper, as if he has walked, smiled, and chatted with them. To take his leave of *La bohème* and abandon this world whose life they had shared as friends must surely have had a melancholy effect on Puccini's spirit, as well as on that of his preferred costumier. Hohenstein's dress designs for the character of Tosca were inspired by the haughty personality of Sarah Bernhardt, whose performance in the play of the same name by Victorien Sardou had so enraptured Puccini. Though at Milan's Teatro Filodrammatici in 1890 the composer could have understood only a few words, he had applauded La Bernhardt enthusiastically. On the stage of Rome's Teatro Costanzi, Puccini's *Tosca* (1900) was embodied in the strong features of the Romanian soprano Haricléa Darclée. Hohenstein portrays the heroine making her way to the church of Sant'Andrea della Valle brandishing a walking-stick like a weapon of imperious dominion. The willpower and strength of the character whose every step is an invitation to love has become an icon for the many famous singers who drift onto the stage with a mysterious air worthy of a Hollywood diva: Géraldine Farrar, Mary Garden, Marthe Chenal, Claudia Muzio, Maria Jeritza, Régine Crespin, Renata Tebaldi, Magda Olivero ...

Maria Callas went against this tradition, making her entrance at London's Covent Garden (1964, directed by Franco Zeffirelli) as defenseless and already ill-fated. Less the mistress of the dangerous game of seduction than the plaything of earthly passion, Callas abandoned the masterful air that had delighted audiences at New York's Metropolitan Opera (1956, directed by Dino Yannopoulos). In the new London production, Tosca wore elaborate robes by Marcel Escoffier, but she no longer strode about like a queen, the impression being more that of a spirit in pain. The diva entered the church with a restless look, bearing a disheveled bunch of tulips and zinnias, breathlessly expectant of her lover's ardent embrace and almost oblivious of the fact she is in a holy place. She offers a striking contrast to the calculated impassibility of Baron Scarpia: Tito Gobbi paces with measured steps, analyzing the situation, imposing his will with the implacable discernment of a man accustomed to intrigue. His elegance is devoid of affectation and his perfidious mask as a man of honor is carefully crafted. In some nine hundred performances the famous baritone perfected what was his favorite role, refining details in the make-up and even adopting an artificial aristocratic aquiline nose.[7] The metamorphosis was attained by the simple expedient of wearing less and less eye-catching garments and doing away with all the tail-coats, embroidery, decorations, court-swords, and riding-crops. Hohenstein's turn-of-the-century design for the chief of the Roman police remains an unsurpassed model. The *noir* character of *Tosca* and its dark "powerful shades"[8] is superbly conveyed in the poster drawn by the same Hohenstein that encapsulates the story, the costume ideas, the production, as well as the whole rich brew of blood and passion. The eponymous heroine towers like a praying-mantis over the body of the tyrant brandishing a crucifix: a sensual "extreme unction" plunged into a symbolic, theatrical backdrop dripping red.

Aida, Giuseppe Verdi • Milan, Teatro alla Scala, 1904
• Aida, Acts I and II • Costume design by Attilio Comelli

Aida Scartato

Per la Scala non eseguito

Atto 2°

ATTO I II

AIDA

The Good, the Bad, and the Ugly:
Character and Costume in the Theater of VERDI and PUCCINI

VITTORIA CRESPI MORBIO

Gianni Schicchi, Giacomo Puccini • New York, Metropolitan Opera, 1918
• Gianni Schicchi • Costume design by Caramba (Luigi Sapelli)

Il tabarro, Giacomo Puccini • New York, Metropolitan Opera, 1918
• Michele • Costume design by Caramba (Luigi Sapelli)

VOCI E COSTUMI

The Good, the Bad, and the Ugly:
Character and Costume in the Theater of VERDI and PUCCINI

VITTORIA CRESPI MORBIO

With *Tosca* Hohenstein bid farewell to the stage. The costume design for Puccini's new creation, *Madama Butterfly*, was thus left in the care of Giuseppe Palanti (1881-1946), an artist supported by Giulio Ricordi who had a flair for discovering emerging talent. The young artist was soon turning the painting studies he had recently completed at the Accademia di Brera in Milan, his experience as a textile designer, and his passion for the decorative arts to good use, coming up with a series of kimonos in an attractive range of colors for the procession of Pinkerton's betrothed, delineating the simple furnishings of a Japanese home, and diligently deploying various ideas gleaned from books, photographs, and historical documents. The artist advanced cautiously, avoiding the risk of giving a personality to figures who do little more than wear complicated Oriental garb and typical make-up: blackened teeth and plucked eyebrows for the old mother; a gold silk *obi* a meter wide by three long for Butterfly. Puccini's young fiancée sings heady lines of simulated innocence: "I am the most cheerful child in Japan, indeed in all the world," and Palanti dresses her in a costume as fresh as a spring breeze, stitched with rosettes in relief. The "farce" wedding unmasks the cynical ploy of Pinkerton, who instead dreams of "a real marriage to a real wife ... an American"; in an understated manner, the costumier prefigures the fatalism that concludes with the victim immolating herself in the gruesome ritual of *seppuku* with the design of a butterfly oozing blood in the carmine-colored tassels confined to the costume of a member of the chorus.

Palanti was determined not to tread on the professional toes of Tito Ricordi, the criticized director of the world première, and did little more than parade around some graceful if rigid figures. He proceeded to hone his taste for color in many-hued designs for Oriental garments which neutralized the pale Western-style ensembles sported by Lady Pinkerton. It was Rosina Storchio who supplied that touch of poetry to the character of Butterfly which won Puccini's heart: "I think that Butterfly without Rosina Storchio would be a creature without a soul!"[9] Hohenstein, meanwhile, in what was his last opera poster, offered the maestro a consummate example of dramaturgical synthesis: Butterfly is swallowed up in the chill half-shadow of the room, stretching out her arms towards the little boy bathed in the life-giving rays.

Palanti's idiom took an unexpected turn soon afterward, in the direction of sensual, soft feminine bodies—if possible, without clothing. His masterpiece is a poster designed for Mascagni's *Isabeau* (Teatro Coliseo, Buenos Aires, 1911) whose protagonist, side-saddle on a white stallion, caught the eye of the censor, her body thus hidden beneath long flowing locks. In the theater, Palanti excelled in the repertory of fairyland, in the unreal world of Gluck's *Armida*, or in the morbidly opulent Orient of Strauss's *Salome*. His cheerful optimism was close to that of the idealist school of fantastical and unbuttoned artists headed by Edel, a group that also included Attilio Comelli (1858-1925), English born but Italian by adoption. The hundredth anniversary of Verdi's birth offered Comelli the opportunity of staging a scrupulously Egyptian *Aida*, underpinned by recent archeological findings and exuding a heady whiff of Art Deco (Teatro alla Scala, 1913).

The costumier shuttled back and forth between London and Milan, where in the same year he was called upon to work on a demanding new version of *Nabucco*. A mature artist and a consummate draftsman, Comelli's brush brought forth Aida, Amneris, priestesses, and commoners, with the relaxed pose of exquisite mannequins bedecked in Egyptian-style garb. Such charm and freedom found their justification in a change in patron: Verdi and Giulio Ricordi, who had died in 1912, were succeeded by a new generation of backers eager for productions that would bowl their audiences over, genuine theatrical blockbusters. Thus costumiers were faced with a new task: no longer to explore the psychology of the characters, but to paint fantastical historical ensembles. As in a mosaic, a costume becomes a fragment of a theatrical fresco intended to make a great visual impact.

Even Arrigo Boito, the librettist of *Otello* and *Falstaff*, who grew up with Verdi's work and understood it, entrusted his *Nerone* (text and music by Boito) to the sculptor Lodovico Pogliaghi, burdening him with an unconscionable amount of researching and ferreting in archives that dragged on for decades. The libretto was published in 1901 but the opera only reached the stage in 1924, a memorial to an artist who had passed away six years previously and to whom La Scala felt a huge debt. As one would expect, Toscanini followed the author's demands to the letter in a spectacular production of exorbitant expense: "Perhaps it was exaggerated, but it all was prescribed in the stage directions [...] either it would have to be played like an oratorio, or else one had just to do it like that."[10]

Gabriele d'Annunzio too waxed lyrical in detailed and verbose directions for the musical dramas of Riccardo Zandonai (*Francesca da Rimini*), Alberto Franchetti (*La figlia di Jorio*), Italo Montemezzi (*La nave*), Ildebrando Pizzetti (*Fedra*), Pietro Mascagni (*Parisina*), Claude Debussy (*Le Martyre de Saint-Sébastien*),

La traviata, Giuseppe Verdi • Milan, Teatro alla Scala, 1906
• Violetta, Act I • Costume design by Caramba (Luigi Sapelli)

The Good, the Bad, and the Ugly:
Character and Costume in the Theater of VERDI and PUCCINI

VOCI E COSTUMI

VITTORIA CRESPI MORBIO

Turandot, Giacomo Puccini • Rome, Teatro Costanzi, 1926
• Turandot, Act II • Costume design by Umberto Brunelleschi

Turandot, Giacomo Puccini • Rome, Teatro Costanzi, 1926
• Seductress of the sultan Calif, Act III • Costume design by Umberto Brunelleschi

The Good, the Bad, and the Ugly:
Character and Costume in the Theater of VERDI and PUCCINI

VITTORIA CRESPI MORBIO

and Arthur Honegger (*Phaedra*). Playing an active role in productions of his stage works, d'Annunzio opted for the incisive synthesis that was the hallmark of renowned painters such as Adolfo De Carolis (1874-1928), Pietro Marussig (1879-1937), and Duilio Cambellotti (1876-1960). On paper the costumes acquire their own character, immersed in a climate of poetic archaism, but on stage there prevails a realistic verisimilitude down to authentic farmhouse furniture and red roses, while the blood was freshly supplied by the still warm bodies of chickens that had laid down their lives for the love of art.

One of d'Annunzio's collaborators was Luigi Sapelli, who signed himself Caramba (1865-1936), not a painter by profession, but a brilliant costumier with an unquestionable talent for the theater. The artist remains more closely associated with Puccini, for whom he completed stage designs for the Italian première of *La rondine* (Teatro Comunale, Bologna, 1917), having designed costumes for the world première of *Il trittico* (Metropolitan Opera, 1918). In a fresh style inherited from early years as a cartoonist and caricaturist, and with a note of kindly sympathy Caramba brings to life the monastic microcosm of *Suor Angelica* and illuminates the craggy features of the sly Gianni Schicchi. His Michele in *Il tabarro* sports a coat apparently stained with the gloomy waters of the Seine, the color of night, of happiness lost, of death. Caramba manages to reconcile a respect for the will of Verdi and Puccini with his own fertile imagination. In a new version of *La traviata* Violetta divested herself of the curious "à la Richelieu" garb in which she appeared at Venice's Teatro la Fenice in 1853, and was transformed into a head-turning *prima donna* complete with ermine-trimmed décolleté (Teatro alla Scala, 1906). Finally the fallen woman could display the attire of a lady of the mid-19th century without causing a fuss: nevertheless, the free-and-easy air given her by the costumier made her familiar to many a debutante of the early 20th century.

Beginning in 1923, Caramba was promoted to the post of productions director at La Scala: costume design now formed part of a more complex scheme comprising lighting, stage business, and a range of sets and backdrops. A friend of the librettist Giuseppe Adami, and with encouragement from Arturo Toscanini, Caramba managed to get his own costumes accepted for the long-awaited production of *Turandot* at La Scala in 1926, two years after Puccini's demise. The earlier designs for that opera, commissioned from Umberto Brunelleschi (1879-1949) by Puccini himself, made an appearance at the Rome production staged later that year at the Teatro Costanzi. A resident of Paris, Brunelleschi proved less of an innovator than a fashionable artist: his clever costume designs fuse elements from Erté and Persian miniature, evincing an erotic (albeit chaste) undertone that provides a foretaste of his success as an illustrator of Giacomo Casanova and Pierre Louÿs. Caramba, however, did not find time to work up the sketches he had produced for *Turandot*: painting directly on to the material, the colors are boldly juxtaposed with a mix of highly disparate fabrics coming together under the artificial glare of the footlights. The result is amazingly modern, a fireworks display that indeed made the opera look "unusual and original,"[11] in accordance with Puccini's dying wish.

Tosca, Giacomo Puccini • Rome, Teatro Costanzi, 1900 • Description of the characters for the papal procession ("Te Deum"), Act I

Descrizione dei Figurini

№ 1.	Piffero Svizzero e Tamburrino	— Tutto di lanetta amaranto a fascie ro di lana bianca — Cappello di feltro a sinistra — piegatura altissima — penn e rosse — Grande fascia amaranto or co per sorreggere la sciabola.
2.	Sargente Svizzero	— Calzoni e calzette lana rosso scarla ni a strisce ribboccate — abito lana lato in bianco — grande fascia nera gere la spada diritta — cappello fe ne — bastone nero con pomo d'oro scollo a doppia riga
3.	Sergente Svizzero in corazza	— Come il № 2 più la corazza e l' la corazza la grande fascia nera ge la spada — il bastone
4.	Ufficiale svizzero	— Calzoni a strisce ribboccate lana riflessi in raso nero — sotto la corazza ticciola a strisce pendenti — calze ner turo completo con arabeschi dorati — scollo — bastone
5	Soldato Svizzero	— Calze, calzoni, corpetto a larghe strisce bleu in lana corazza e alabarda (non elmo — Preferirei il piccolo al figurino № più caratteristico — cappello feltro come il Sarg
6	Idem	

RAPPRESENTAZIONE

The Composer Paints:
VERDI, PUCCINI, and Their Scenic Worlds

ROGER PARKER

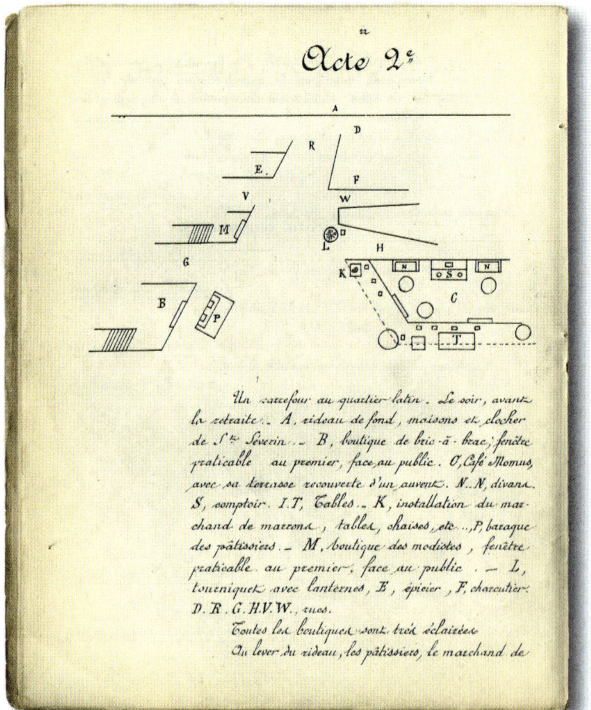
22

Acte 2e

Un carrefour au quartier latin. Le soir, avant la retraite. – A, rideau de fond, maisons et clocher de Ste Séverin. – B, boutique de bric-à-brac; fenêtre praticable au premier, face au public. C, Café Momus, avec sa terrasse recouverte d'un auvent. N..N, divans. S, comptoir. I.T, Tables. – K, installation du marchand de marrons, tables, chaises, etc.., P, baraque des pâtissiers. – M, boutique des modistes, fenêtre praticable au premier, face au public. – L, tourniquet avec lanternes, E, épicier, F, charcutier. D. R. G. H.V.W., rues.

Toutes les boutiques sont très éclairées

Au lever du rideau, les pâtissiers, le marchand de

La bohème, Giacomo Puccini • Paris, Opéra-Comique, 1898 • *Mise en scène* written by Albert Carré

The Composer Paints: VERDI, PUCCINI, and Their Scenic Worlds

ROGER PARKER

Imagine the following: You are fortunate enough to attend performances of Verdi's Aida *in London, Milan, and New York. The performances are all different—different casts, conductors, orchestras, staging teams; but you have expectations of both difference and sameness.*

You will expect the singers, despite their individual quirks, to sing a more-or-less identical literary and musical text. True, a high note here or there may be added to showcase a particular singer, and—more often than one might think—there may be a discreet transposition of a key to ease the depredations of age or nerves that afflict other singers; but these are matters of small detail. You will trust that the conductor and orchestral musicians have identical parts before them—although, yet again, conductors will routinely adjust details to suit the theatrical space and thus aid audibility. Some performances may even choose to substitute rejected fragments in order to renew the text. For example, Verdi wrote a full-scale overture for *Aida*, and then discarded it at the dress rehearsals of the opera's first performances in Milan in 1872, deciding that his prelude was better; we might like to try out the overture in an occasional performance, if only to assure ourselves that Verdi was right. But again, these are details.

What, though, of the *staging* of these three productions? Your expectations of sameness in that area will, if you are at all experienced as an opera-goer, be of the most modest imaginable. In London the scenery and costumes have been created by a famous fashion designer, whose name on the poster is placed in much larger letters than those of the composer—in an effort to attract a younger audience and thus fend off endless complaints about state-subsidized opera being "elitist." In Milan there is a fabulously expensive recreation of ancient Egypt, with real horses pulling real carriages in the triumphal procession, and huge vistas everywhere. And in New York the staging is what die-hards proudly call "traditional," which means that it looks about the same as it would have when the people bankrolling the production were young enough to enjoy newness: a kind of mid-twentieth-century pastiche or—more accurately—a mid-century directorial style frozen in aspic.

But now imagine a different world, one in which—through some unimaginable warp in our present civilization—the staging world is as relatively fixed as the musical or literary one. In just the same way as there is a libretto and a musical score, there is now a "production book" that tells us exactly how to stage *Aida*: what the sets and costumes should look like, who stands where, even what gestures they are permitted to make. As with the musical performance, relatively tiny variations or inflections can now give pleasure or cause indignation. "Look! How expressive and daring! Radames is wearing *mauve* tights tonight instead of *red* ones! I'm not sure what it *means* exactly; but somehow it seemed to fit marvelously with that slightly off-color drapery at the back of the Act I set. At the end of his aria, though, did you

Falstaff, Giuseppe Verdi • Milan, Teatro alla Scala, 1893
• Emma Zilli in the role of Alice Ford

Milano 10/3/93

GIULIO ROSSI

(Souvenir de Alice Ford)
All'Ill.ma Sig.a Contessa Giulia Ricordi
la riconoscentissima
Emma Zilli

The Composer Paints: VERDI, PUCCINI, and Their Scenic Worlds

ROGER PARKER

notice that he raised *both* hands when launching his final high note? Now really that goes too far. He looked like he was parking an airplane. The text stipulates quite clearly that his other hand should be resting on his sword at this point, and there's a very good reason why it should. These modern directors! Sharpen up my quill pen: I must write a letter to *Opera News*."

The imaginary landscape I've just painted, one in which what we might call "same-staging practice" is the norm, is of course fantastic: a kind of *Groundhog Day* made opera, in which the same actions will scroll past us again and again—more like a movie rerun than "live" theatre. But I conjure it up because doing so may confront us with something important about our present-day attitudes to staging. To ask a very obvious question: Is an "authentic" staging ever possible? Can the composer's intentions be respected so far as this aspect of the operatic event is concerned? As most of these works were created before the days of film, it might seem obvious that we can't: that the evidence of what happened on stage, and thus—although this is a big additional step—of what Verdi wanted in *Aida*, simply doesn't exist. But, as so often, the 19th- and early 20th-century past, with its bewildering abundance of documentary witnesses, can surprise us. In this case it can demonstrate that composers of this period had a considerable effect on, and were considerably affected by, the visual aspect of the works they created. This essay will explore some of the ramifications of this, and will begin by looking at its most obvious textual manifestation.

Scholars and (some) opera producers have long known about the presence of 19th-century operatic production books, documents that attempt to notate, sometimes in great detail, the visual side of opera: where the characters should stand, what movements they should make, what they should wear, what the scenery should look like. The French, who invented them, called them *livrets de mise en scène*, and their purpose was to ensure that operatic productions in the provinces and elsewhere would follow the way things had been done in Paris, where immense care was taken over every detail of operatic staging. The Italians, who imported the idea later in the century, called them *disposizioni sceniche*. Verdi, who throughout his life took a keen interest in all aspects of operatic staging, was a prime force in the Italian adoption of the practice. He had experienced them in Paris with his *Grand-opéra Les Vêpres siciliennes* (1855); and then, starting with *Un ballo in maschera* (1859), he tried to persuade his Italian collaborators to use them whenever possible, and was closely involved in the creation of several of them. These production books (both in France and Italy) lasted into the early years of the twentieth century, but then mostly died out, replaced by photographs, film, and other means of recording performance. There have been some interesting speculations about how their instructions might be transferred to the modern stage, and even a few brave attempts at following them in detail. But these days we above all prefer novelty in stage performance: *Groundhog Day* at the opera is a long way off.

It is now something of a commonplace that the production books coincided with, and were inseparably linked to, the Europe-wide establishment of what we now call repertory opera, the gradual formation of an operatic world based not on the constant production of new works, but on the revival of past classics. This was a fundamental shift in values, one that affected almost all aspects of operatic production; and of course it is still very much with us today. It changed the way in which composers and librettists thought of themselves as creators, and of the relative status of their works in the artistic pantheon; it also changed

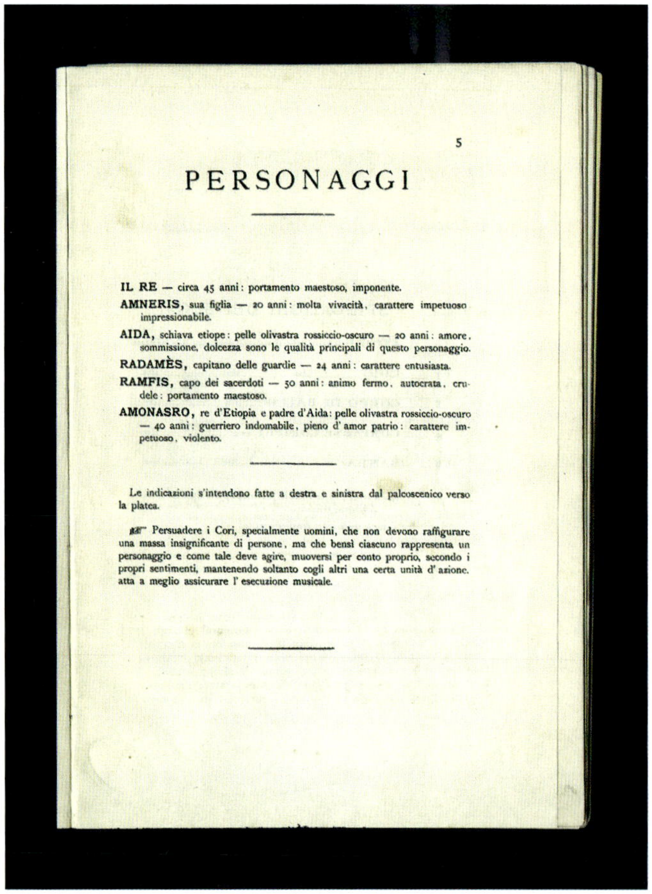

5

PERSONAGGI

IL RE — circa 45 anni: portamento maestoso, imponente.

AMNERIS, sua figlia — 20 anni: molta vivacità, carattere impetuoso impressionabile.

AIDA, schiava etiope: pelle olivastra rossiccio-oscuro — 20 anni: amore, sommissione, dolcezza sono le qualità principali di questo personaggio.

RADAMÈS, capitano delle guardie — 24 anni: carattere entusiasta.

RAMFIS, capo dei sacerdoti — 50 anni: animo fermo, autocrata, crudele: portamento maestoso.

AMONASRO, re d'Etiopia e padre d'Aida: pelle olivastra rossiccio-oscuro — 40 anni: guerriero indomabile, pieno d' amor patrio: carattere impetuoso, violento.

Le indicazioni s'intendono fatte a destra e sinistra dal palcoscenico verso la platea.

☞ Persuadere i Cori, specialmente uomini, che non devono raffigurare una massa insignificante di persone, ma che bensì ciascuno rappresenta un personaggio e come tale deve agire, muoversi per conto proprio, secondo i propri sentimenti, mantenendo soltanto cogli altri una certa unità d' azione. atta a meglio assicurare l' esecuzione musicale.

Aida, Giuseppe Verdi • Milan, Teatro alla Scala, 1872
• *Disposizione scenica* compiled and edited by Giulio Ricordi, 1873
• Description of the main characters

their attitudes to the balance between convention and originality, with the latter increasingly seen as a necessary artistic goal; and it changed singing style, favoring as it did those most able to adapt to a broader, more cosmopolitan repertory. But most obviously the shift called into question what has become for us, existing as we do at an extreme point in this continuing process of repertory formation, that crucial aesthetic issue surrounding the visual aspect of opera: When revivals of a classic work are mounted, how far should the original staging of that work be considered part of its basic text? In other words, how far is that first staging to be regarded as "authentic"—on a par with the words and music? The appearance of the production books reflects what most today would see as a radically restrictive answer to these questions.

This is not to suggest that before the time of the production books, which means in Verdi's case before *Les Vêpres siciliennes*, the composer had little to do with staging. Far from it: there is every evidence that Verdi cared about it passionately from his earliest days, even though he could sometimes do little to control the details. In Italian opera during the years of Verdi's early successes there was no such thing as the modern "stage director." As we have seen elsewhere in this volume, scenery was of great importance, and in the best theaters was entrusted to artists of great repute; but details of staging were usually the responsibility of the librettist (or a local substitute); and from the evidence we have, this was mostly a case of making sure that the chorus moved about sensibly and that ensemble scenes were sensibly blocked. The soloists would reckon to bring their own gestures (in the early days, gestures drawn from a library of stock poses understood to represent the various emotions), and would tend to move about much less frequently than modern singers. Often, the quality of the staging

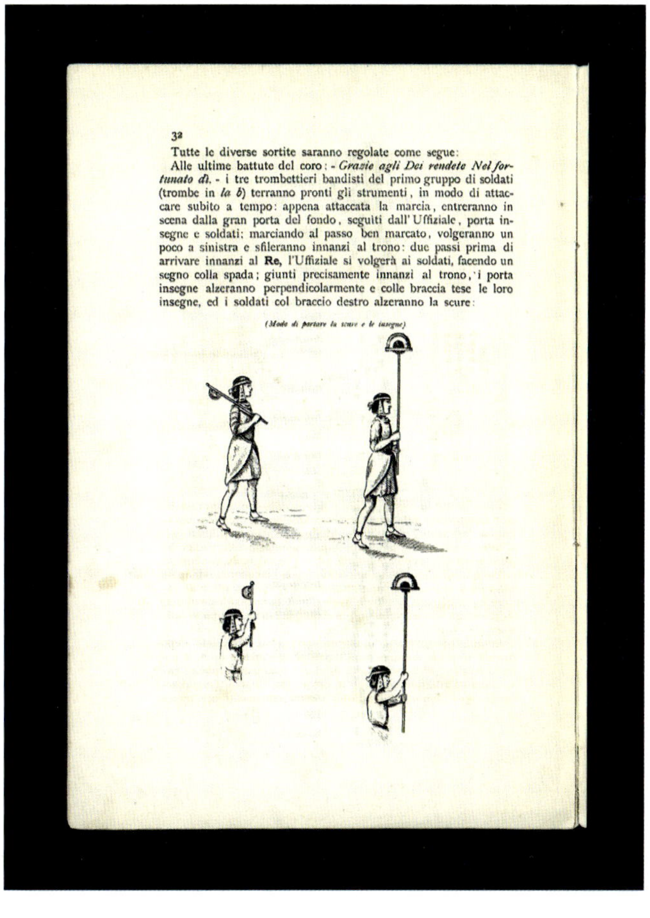
32

Tutte le diverse sortite saranno regolate come segue:

Alle ultime battute del coro: - *Grazie agli Dei rendete Nel fortunato dì.* - i tre trombettieri bandisti del primo gruppo di soldati (trombe in *la b*) terranno pronti gli strumenti, in modo di attaccare subito a tempo: appena attaccata la marcia, entreranno in scena dalla gran porta del fondo, seguiti dall'Uffiziale, porta insegne e soldati; marciando al passo ben marcato, volgeranno un poco a sinistra e sfileranno innanzi al trono: due passi prima di arrivare innanzi al **Re,** l'Uffiziale si volgerà ai soldati, facendo un segno colla spada; giunti precisamente innanzi al trono, i porta insegne alzeranno perpendicolarmente e colle braccia tese le loro insegne, ed i soldati col braccio destro alzeranno la scure:

(Modo di portare la scure e le insegne)

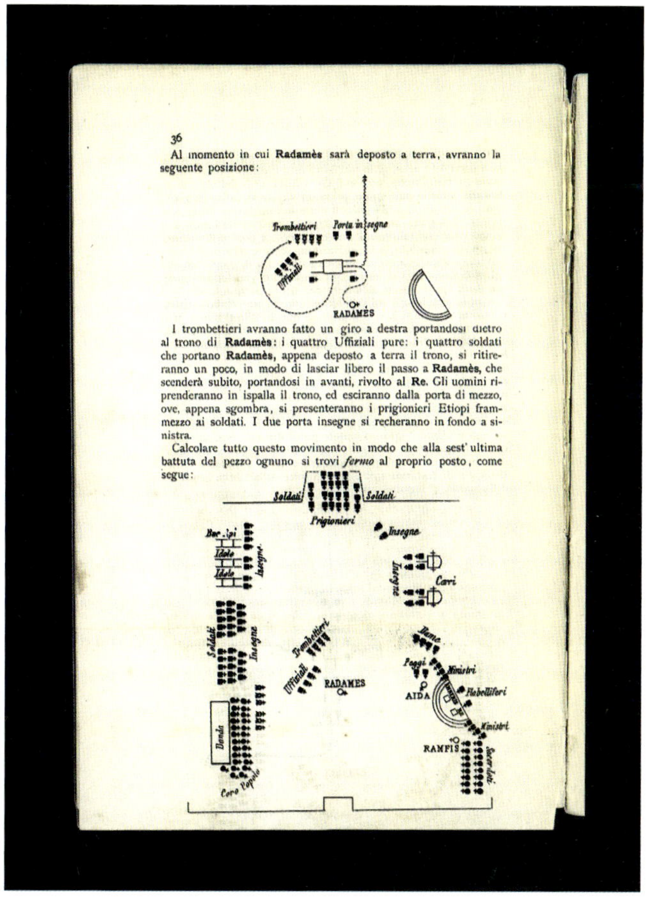
36

Al momento in cui **Radamès** sarà deposto a terra, avranno la seguente posizione:

I trombettieri avranno fatto un giro a destra portandosi dietro al trono di **Radamès**: i quattro Uffiziali pure: i quattro soldati che portano **Radamès,** appena deposto a terra il trono, si ritireranno un poco, in modo di lasciar libero il passo a **Radamès,** che scenderà subito, portandosi in avanti, rivolto al **Re.** Gli uomini riprenderanno in ispalla il trono, ed esciranno dalla porta di mezzo, ove, appena sgombra, si presenteranno i prigionieri Etiopi frammezzo ai soldati. I due porta insegne si recheranno in fondo a sinistra.

Calcolare tutto questo movimento in modo che alla sest'ultima battuta del pezzo ognuno si trovi *fermo* al proprio posto, come segue:

Aida, Giuseppe Verdi • Milan, Teatro alla Scala, 1872
• *Disposizione scenica* compiled and edited by Giulio Ricordi, 1873
• Men bearing martial insignia for the triumphal march

Aida, Giuseppe Verdi • Milan, Teatro alla Scala, 1872
• *Disposizione scenica* compiled and edited by Giulio Ricordi, 1873
• Arrival of Radames after the Egyptian victory

The Composer Paints:
VERDI, PUCCINI, and Their Scenic Worlds

ROGER PARKER

had something to do with the reputation of the composer: Verdi, in his later reminiscences (if we can trust them, which in many cases we can't), mentions that his first great success, *Nabucco* (1842), risked failure because, as he had virtually no reputation, it was thrown together quickly, making use of old stage sets. However, and within these constraints, the young Verdi was as demanding as he could be.

In the later stages of his career, when he was unquestionably Italy's most famous opera composer, all this had changed. Especially after the impact of his various sojourns in Paris, the staging of each new opera would be the cause of endless discussions, in many of which the composer joined with the usual passion. *Aida* is a prime example. In Verdi's very first letter about the brief *scenario* that would eventually blossom into the *Aida* libretto, he announced that "I have read the Egyptian outline. It is well done; it offers a splendid *mise en scène*, and there are two or three situations which, if not very new, are certainly very beautiful." Here his priorities are very clear: first comes the *mise en scène* (and it is significant that Verdi uses the French term here), the opportunities presented in the *scenario* for variation of setting and a series of striking visual pictures; and then come the "situations," the opportunities for characters to confront one another against these various backdrops. It is clear in other words that, at this early stage of the project, the scenic possibilities were of paramount importance, and indissolubly linked to the other possibilities of the plot.

As it happens, one of the most interesting early letters about *Aida* and its staging is not by Verdi, but raises an issue which became especially important to the later 19th century, and which had been a recurring problem in opera from its very first days: that of realism. In one sense, of course, opera had always been inherently unrealistic: characters sing rather than speak. But it seems that each new operatic generation had to wrestle anew with the problems this created, resolving it with fresh compromises. The particular tension in the later 19th century focused on the business of visual authenticity: the fact that new archeological and historical researches had made it possible to recreate all sorts of costumes from the past. But how would these be integrated into opera? The letter in question comes from Auguste Mariette, the French Egyptologist who had written that first *scenario*, and is addressed to the head of the opera house in Cairo, where *Aida* was to have its world première:

> It is in the costumes, above all, that we shall encounter difficulty. To create imaginary Egyptians as they are usually seen in the theater is not difficult; and if nothing else were needed, I would not be involved. But to unite in proper measure the ancient costumes shown in the temples and the requirements of the modern stage constitutes a delicate task. A king may be quite handsome in granite with an enormous crown on his head. But when it comes to dressing one of flesh and bone and making him walk and sing ... that becomes embarrassing and, it is to be feared, makes people laugh.

There, in a nutshell, is the eternal problem of opera: the more realistic you make the sets and the costumes, the greater the risk that your real-life actors, walking around the stage and singing at the tops of their voices, will seem simply out of place. Then as now, the delicate balance that all opera producers face every day of their professional lives must be struck.

As mentioned, Verdi often had firm views about these matters, but in the end was typically pragmatic. When offered a choice between various set designs, he would invariably choose the least cluttered—in other words, the one that would ensure that the characters, the singing actors, would stand out most clearly. And although he showed some considerable enthusiasm for authentic Egyptian instruments, he made sure that adjustments would be possible in order that they could play the very modern range of notes he had envisaged for them. But his greatest concern was for the movements of the actors on stage, and in particular how these would articulate the very precise fluctuations in mood that he had written into his music. Nowhere is this more evident than in the string of innovative duets that he sprinkled through *Aida*, and nowhere is the *disposizione scenica* for *Aida* more revealing of precisely what Verdi required. In almost all cases, these duets move through contrasting musical movements, some of which are filled with stage action, others of which are dedicated to lyrical reflection; and it is clear from the *disposizione scenica* that the actions of singers on stage were minutely plotted against this broad alternation, with significant changes of position and fluidity in the action sections, and comparative stasis in the lyrical ones. Could such instructions be transferred to the modern stage? It seems unlikely, in that we 21st-century viewers, brought up as we are on film and television, are used to a degree of visual activity that would have been considered highly distracting in the 19th century. Again, the fraught issue of realism, or, more precisely, of shifting perceptions of realism, is at stake.

We know that a *disposizione scenica* for Verdi's final opera, *Falstaff* (1893), existed, but unfortunately no copy seems to have

La bohème, Giacomo Puccini • Ascribed to Turin, Teatro Regio, 1896 • Mimì and Rodolfo in the garret, Act I • Photograph of the staging

La bohème, Giacomo Puccini • Ascribed to Turin, Teatro Regio, 1896 • Marcello, Mimì, Rodolfo, and Musetta at the Barrière d'Enfer, Act III • Photograph of the staging

The Composer Paints: VERDI, PUCCINI, and Their Scenic Worlds

ROGER PARKER

Tosca, Giacomo Puccini • Interior of Sant'Andrea della Valle, Act I
• Photograph of the staging, early 20th century

Tosca, Giacomo Puccini • On the platform of Castel Sant'Angelo after Cavaradossi's execution, Act III • Photograph of the staging, early 20th century

The Composer Paints: VERDI, PUCCINI, and Their Scenic Worlds

ROGER PARKER

survived. However, we can be sure from the voluminous correspondence related to the opera that the issues of authenticity and realism continued to arise. We know, for example, that the set designer, Adolf Hohenstein, went to London and Windsor to research appropriate sets, and also that he found in the British Museum evidence about the way people might dress at the time of Henry IV. What is more, we can see from early costume designs that in some respects these researches were taken through into the first performance. But the overwhelming impression of an opera such as *Falstaff*, which everyone at the time knew was probably Verdi's last major work and was thus a part of music history even while it was being written, was how huge and dauntingly complex an undertaking it was. The aging Verdi was vividly aware of this, but nevertheless took an active interest in the visual as well as the musical side. He forcibly expressed his views on the former to his publisher Giulio Ricordi, in a letter written some months before the première. The composer's sentiments are typical in their general desire, mentioned earlier, to favor comparatively simple scenic options that would allow the characters to stand out clearly, but he also betrays the fact that his mid-century enthusiasm for the Parisian ways of doing things had cooled somewhat:

> The more we proceed, the more complicated things become. [...] What do we need to do now about costume designs, about sets, etc., etc.? Let's not look for too much! We have two choices: either a *mise en scène* after the [Paris] *Opéra* fashion (they cost from two to three hundred thousand francs), or an unpretentious *mise en scène* (which is better) [...]. In Italy things must be done cheaply, and without pretense, and without looking for *midi à quatorze heures*.

Whether he got his way must be judged by the eventual set designs; but, as with *Aida*, one can be sure that Verdi's major efforts so far as *mise en scène* were concerned were directed towards the singers, and in particular towards their actions on stage. Near the time of the *Falstaff* première, Giulio Ricordi published a fascinating account of how Verdi went about rehearsing: in particular how, at this late stage in his career, he took upon himself the task that today would be the province of the "director." Ricordi emphasized above all that Verdi felt it was part of his brief to ensure that the gestures and movements of the actors were rigorously connected to the music they sang. When he felt something was lacking, if a move or gesture did not satisfy him, then he himself became the character, declaiming and singing to show exactly how to interpret a role. For him, one would guess, there was little essentially different between musical declamation and the gestures that accompanied them: each was intended to produce nothing other than the maximum theatrical effect.

Giacomo Puccini's first operas were produced in very similar circumstances to Verdi's last: indeed, the younger composer's first great success, *Manon Lescaut* (1893), was premièred a matter of days before *Falstaff* and, because it was also masterminded by the Ricordi publishing firm, seemed to have been created almost in tandem with it. *Manon* also gave rise to an impressively detailed *disposizione scenica* (copies of which have survived), one very similar to Verdi's later ones in its enormous accumulation of detail. None of his later operas have quite such an authoritative document tied to their first performances (as mentioned earlier, the vogue for production books faded in the early years of the 20th century), but we nevertheless have an enormous amount of information to attest to the fact that Puccini cared deeply about how his operas were staged. It should come as no surprise, though, that the difficulties of stage realism which hover over Verdi's last works become, if anything, even more fraught in the case of the younger composer.

This much can be seen in the genesis of each of the next three operas. In the case of *La bohème* (1896), the central, at times acrimonious argument between the composer and his librettists was about scenic matters: at heart about whether there

Madama Butterfly, Giacomo Puccini • New York, Metropolitan Opera, 1905 • Cio-Cio-San and her friends • Photograph of the staging should be an act in the courtyard of Musetta's apartment, one culminating in an elaborate improvised party. Eventually, and in spite of the fact that the entire act had been written by his long-suffering librettists, Puccini decided that this innovative scenic idea had to be jettisoned: one assumes because he could not find a sufficiently strong musical color to match the visual effect. This sense in which Puccini gained vital musical inspiration (or not) from a visual ambience is repeated again and again during the frequently tortured progress he made towards his operas' final shapes, and was also, in many cases, a cause of initial confusion on the part of those who first witnessed the finished product. For example, the music of the second act of *La bohème*, which takes place outside the Café Momus, is plainly a kind of aural counterpart to the riot of visual detail that the setting and its action proposed, with its urban bustle and hectic action and alluring nocturnal colors. Several early critics even voiced a concern that the sheer proliferation of musical detail had damagingly fragmented Puccini's lyrical impulses (a complaint that turned

Madama Butterfly, Giacomo Puccini • New York, Metropolitan Opera, 1905 • Uncle Bonzo repudiates Cio-Cio-San • Photograph of the staging

Falstaff, Giuseppe Verdi • Verdi and the singers during rehearsal
• Drawing by Adolf Hohenstein, 1893

out to be a common theme among early reactions to his operas). Such a complaint is difficult for us to understand. The opera is now so well known that we can understand and take pleasure in the small moments of lyrical pause that Puccini injects into his score: but it is good to be reminded that his desire to be realistic was, for his first critics and audiences, often confusing.

Nowhere was this confusion more evident than in the reaction to Puccini's next opera, *Tosca* (1900), in which the precise ambience—three historical sites in Rome in 1800, during Napoleonic times—proved to be a central feature of the musical character. Obviously a degree of strictly visual authenticity was now expected. Puccini had several meetings with the author of the original play, the Frenchman Victorien Sardou, and was amused to find that the playwright had imagined a magnificent backcloth in which Rome's Tiber would be shown flowing between St. Peter's and the Castel Sant'Angelo (these buildings are in fact on the same side of the river). More importantly, though, critics again pounced on the musical authenticity, remarking—often in negative terms—that much of the opera is invaded by realistic sounds: gunshots, off-stage music, religious chants, and above all the pealing of bells. Again, Puccini's inspiration seems to have come directly from the ambience: he researched extensively the exact pitch of certain Roman bells, in order that their intrusion could have the maximum authenticity; but, more than this, he then allowed bell-like sounds to infiltrate many of the more lyrical musical moments, such as the great soliloquy for the villain Scarpia that closes Act I, which is underpinned by a constant, tolling oscillation of two bell-like sounds.

If anything, this pattern intensified with *Madama Butterfly* (1904), in which strict authenticity was not such a requirement (the setting in Japan was very distant to most people, and when Puccini borrowed actual Japanese melodies he made no attempt to use them in ways appropriate to their origins). But again, matters of scenic ambience were crucial to the overall structure. Puccini's first idea was to make a long two-act opera in which the first would be set in North America and the second in Japan. This (like so many other first Puccinian inspirations) eventually proved unworkable, but the opera's music continued to rest on a constant oscillation between Western and Eastern musical spheres, as if that first inspiration of scenic alternation had indeed permanently captured his musical imagination.

That final image, of Puccini the musician dictated by the visual impressions he and his collaborators had invented, is a good one on which to end this brief survey. The visual aspect of opera has, since the genre's very first years at the start of the 17th century, always been an important part of the art form's total effect. Indeed, for much of opera's history, scenic splendor has been at least as important as musical ingenuity. But the balance gradually changed in the 19th century: as opera became increasingly seen as essentially a musical genre, so composers began to take more and more interest in scenic elements, using them to bind together and make sense of their increasingly complex sonic inventions. This trend came to a head towards the end of Verdi's life, and during Puccini's. Both composers thus became intimately connected to, and involved with, the visual side of the works they helped to create. This meant that they could sometimes, if they chose, dictate what the scene painters and costume designers should do; but more often it meant that they themselves became musical painters, sonic illustrators of the mysterious, exotic worlds in which opera resides, and—just as important—musical choreographers, imagining a tune through which the characters on stage could then express themselves, not only in song but also in gesture.

Giuseppe Verdi, Letter to Giulio Ricordi • Sant'Agata, 10 July 1871
• Verdi writing about the orchestra which should be "invisible" ➛

sonorità, e per l'effetto. Queste [illegible]menti apriranno poi la strada ad altre innovazioni che verranno certamente un giorno; e fra queste, quella „di togliere dal palco scenico i palchetti degli spettatori, portando il sipario alla ribalta: l'altra, „di rendere l'orchestra invisibile" Quest'idea non è mia, è di Wagner: è buonissima. Sembra impossibile che al giorno d'oggi si tolleri di vedere il nostro meschino *frack*, e le cravatte bianche, miste per es: ad un costume Egizio, Assiro, Druidico etc. etc.; e di vedere, inoltre, la massa d'orchestra, „che è parte del mondo fittizio" quasi nel mezzo della platea fra il mondo dei fischianti, o dei plaudenti. Aggiungete a tutto questo lo sconcio di vedere per aria la testa delle arpe, i manichi dei contrabassi, ed il molinello del Direttore d'orchestra.

Rispondetemi dunque in modo categorico e decisivo perchè se non mi si potesse concedere quanto domando sarebbe inutile continuare in queste trattative — —

Addio.

G. Verdi

EXCURSUS

Metaphor as a way of understanding the culture of a nation

In any group of people, culture is comprised of values, beliefs, rituals, ceremonies, attitudes, and ways of life. These are, however, difficult to put over as concepts, since the dynamics of a culture are for the most part intangible, immaterial, and hard to convey in written form. The Dutch anthropologist Gert Hofstede explains how culture is like a cloud: it hangs over a community and conditions the precipitation that falls on the population below, but if ever we try to touch it, comprised as it is of just gas, it just slips through our fingers. If then the definition and interpretation of the culture of a group is a complex exercise, attempting to account for the culture of an entire nation is far more so. Practically impossible, one might say. And instead, as in all elaborate arguments, idioms do exist that might prove useful. One of these forms is the metaphor. A metaphor is in fact a construct that simplifies complexity and, through a single image, can encapsulate a host of characteristics that would otherwise be tricky to define, by taking advantage of the succinct powers of analogy: "Mark swims like a fish" or "The service offered by that firm is as punctual as a Swiss train."

When it comes to illustrating a national culture, metaphor acts as a guide, a map, a beacon that helps those ignorant of a country to quickly grasp what it is that the members of that society consider most important. Such knowledge ought to allow us to deepen our understanding of international differences (the cross-cultural perspective) and therefore avoid committing "cultural blunders." Obviously, since these metaphors are, from the cognitive point of view, schematically reductive, they can end up stereotyping the relevant concepts and spawning a half-baked appreciation of the phenomena concerned. It is of course obvious that a sophisticated observer would reject the idea that everyone in the Balkans whistles the Klezmer music of the Gipsy Kings or that Swedes invariably round off their supper of smoked herring with a glass of the hard stuff, but the method nonetheless offers a serviceable, coherent image in less refined analytical approaches that are designed to bring out what members of a given community consider most significant, and so steer clear of slip-ups and superficial misreadings.

A stereotype is in fact a mental image of a group and its salient characteristics that each of us has constructed and on the basis of which we attempt to gauge the individuals belonging to the group. It can also easily be misguided and lead to erroneous conclusions. Nonetheless all human beings make use of stereotypes because they provide a ready way of classifying the wealth of stimuli to which we are subjected.

Most of us feel so extremely negative about stereotypes that to be accused of using one can be galling. Yet, if they are employed descriptively rather than as value judgments, stereotypes can be legitimate and may be considered as providing a provisional picture, one based on the information acquired from observation and thus subject to modification if and when new data are acquired. A metaphor may therefore help us understand a country in terms of its history and lifestyle as well as its manner of conducting business.

This method has been employed by an American social scientist, Martin Gannon, professor at the University of Maryland, who fifteen years ago devised an exhaustive research program on cultural metaphor dealing with seventeen countries, including Italy.[1] It is especially pertinent that this view of Italy originates with a foreign analyst who is able, by use of a fresh cognitive template, to produce without prejudice a snapshot of the Italian nation and thus confirm or invalidate the principal preconceptions about the country at large in the international community.

Italy is like a vast lyric opera

In his book Gannon examines various countries, identifying the metaphors that best illustrate the national culture of each. In this analysis, the symbolic representative of France is wine, of Spain, the bullfight, of Germany, the symphony orchestra, of the United States, football (the American variety, obviously), of Sweden, *stuga*, of Belgium, lace, and of Turkey, coffee, and so on. The metaphor for Italy is *opera*—a synthesis of music, dramatic action, pomp, public display, and a sense of destiny. According to our American author, Italians have a tendency to put on a face for outsiders, to enjoy shared experiences, and are accustomed to always being on stage.

The opera in question may be tragic or comic, and intensely personal, with soloists and a chorus who express themselves through words, gestures, and music, and with a consistently high level of performance. Among the seventeen metaphors originally proposed in the first edition of the book, however, that pertaining to Italy might at first glance seem a bit forced and oversimplified. To see Italy portrayed as a caricature of *Cavalleria rusticana* or *Rigoletto* raises a smile. Nonetheless, if one ponders for a while how the metaphor of opera was arrived at, the singular aptness of the comparison begins to dawn on one: Magnificence and grand-standing are hardly alien to Italian daily life, as we can read every day in newspapers and witness in reality-shows on television. Italians who in turn are acquainted with foreign lands and possessed of an aptitude for comparison know full well that the Italian mentality is predicated upon *exteriority*, where emotion is considered to be so strong and predominant that it is thought impossible to conceal it from a third party. Therefore this analogy between the *Bel Paese* and grand opera—an artistic form invented by our forebears and raised to its zenith, and that encapsulates the majority, if not all, the more important positive and negative features of Italian mores—is not so far from the truth.

Even the Italian constitution betrays the importance ascribed to outward impression. In the United States' Declaration of Independence, the first "self-evident" affirmation is that "all men are created equal." In the Italian constitution, the first fundamental principle is that "all citizens should enjoy equal social dignity." The taste for appearances is no less obvious in the way Italians communicate. They tend to be skillful conversation partners and their conversations can be followed at a distance, since whatever they are saying can readily be decoded from their facial expression. This is one of the reasons why, when making a deal, those concerned prefer to talk face to face so they can read every movement in the muscles of their counterpart.

The outward show typical of opera even extends to business matters: When outlining his ideas in the course of a negotiation, a manager pays careful attention to the aesthetic aspect of his presentation, as it provides pointers to his mastery of details and language, as well as to his abilities as an organizer. Refinement and elegance count for a great deal—just like costumes and sets in a theater. Italians speak with passion and rhythm, modulating their tone with frequent episodes of high drama as they talk. It is the quality of one's manner of speaking that possesses the greatest importance—just as in the opera, where the voice register is articulated within a wide range of nuance as the vocal piece unfolds. Between a high and a low tone of voice, Italians have a penchant for the former, turning oral communication into a veritable performance.

For the majority of my fellow countrymen, lively discussion is something of a pastime. Arguments break out everywhere—in bars and cafes, in the office and around the pool table, at condominium leaseholders' meetings, on the radio, even in business contexts, where Italians are far less respectful of hierarchical barriers at work than people in other climes. This lyrical temperament often explodes in highly charged altercations because our emotions seem so strong that it is simply impossible for individuals to hold them in check. This continuous external manifestation of each and every thing of any importance takes place in public and this makes keeping a lid on matters something of a headache. People are forever airing the ins and outs of secret negotiations with friends and family or in the press, the most intimate concerns being laid out for mass consumption. This situation spills over as well into politics, which morphs into an overblown, grandiloquent, and often tub-thumping branch of the entertainment industry.

Born in Italy at the end of the 16th century, opera is a complex and costly affair that for many centuries has surely been one of the best-loved and most idolized forms of theater in our country as well as throughout the world. A slow decline began in the 20th century and it has never regained the popularity of 18th-century melodrama, even though fine works continue to be composed. From the analysis by Gannon referred to above, perhaps it would be useful to unearth material as rich and telling so as to draw out the roots of the Italian people and make them better known even among those with little acquaintance with the country. For the wisdom behind Alfredo's general toast in *La traviata* ("Libiam ne' lieti calici": "Let us drink from the joyous glasses") or Figaro's cavatina "Largo al factotum della città" ("Make way for the jack-of-all-trades of the town") in *Il barbiere di Siviglia* is not merely musical.

It is in music, scenes, costumes, and dances like these that Italian culture resides, laid down over four centuries. One should simply try not to forget it.

APPENDIX

NOTES

Scenography: Prespectives on the Evolution of Operatic Staging

1 *Carteggi pucciniani*, ed. Eugenio Gara (Milano, Ricordi, 1958), letter no. 297.

2 *Carteggi pucciniani*, no. 287; see also *"Madama Butterfly". Fonti e documenti della genesi*, ed. Arthur Groos et al (Lucca, Centro studi Giacomo Puccini, 2005), pp. 115–35, 349.

3 Gaia Piccarolo and Giuliana Ricci, *Luigi Manini (1848–1936) architetto e scenografo, pittore e fotografo* (Crema, Silvana Editoriale – APIC, 2007), p. 48.

4 Franco Abbiati, *Giuseppe Verdi* (Milano, Ricordi, 1959), IV:458–59.

5 Marcello Conati, *La bottega della musica. Verdi e la Fenice* (Milano, Il Saggiatore, 1983), p. 316.

6 *Carteggi pucciniani*, no. 716.

7 *Carteggi pucciniani*, no. 882.

8 *Carteggi pucciniani*, no. 195.

9 "Genesi dell'Aida con documentazione inedita," ed. Saleh Abdoun, in *Quaderni dell'Istituto di studi verdiani* 4 (Parma, 1971), no. 176.

10 Abbiati, IV:433–34.

11 *Carteggi verdiani*, ed. Alessandro Luzio (Roma, Reale Acca demia d'Italia, 1935–1947) I:125.

12 *Carteggi pucciniani*, no. 186.

13 Raphaëlle Legrand and Nicole Wild, *Regards sur l'Opéra-Comique. Trois siècles de vie théâtrale* (Paris, CNRS Éditions, 2002), p. 184.

14 Maria Ida Biggi, Maria Rosaria Corchia, and Viale Ferrero, Mercedes, *Alessandro Sanquirico "il Rossini della pittura sce-nica"* (Pesaro, Fondazione Gioachino Rossini, 2007), pp. XXIX–XXX, XXXIV, *passim*.

15 Reproduced in *"Un ballo in maschera" di Giuseppe Verdi*, with essays by Marinella Pigozzi and David Rosen (Milano, Ricordi, 2002).

16 James A. Hepokoski, and Mercedes Viale Ferrero, *"Otello" di Giuseppe Verdi* (Milano, Ricordi, 1990), p. 10.

17 Filippo Filippi, *Musica e musicisti* (Milano, Libreria Editrice G.Brignola, 1876; reprint of the review of *Aida* from the peri-odical *La Perseveranza*, 1872), p. 372.

18 [Ricordi, Giulio], "Le scene di *Madama Butterfly* al Teatro alla Scala di Milano, in *Musica e musicisti* LIX/3 (March 1904), p. 174.

19 Albert Carré, *Souvenirs de théâtre réunis, présentés et annotés par Robert Favart* (Paris, Librairie Plon, 1950), p. 314.

20 *Carteggi pucciniani*, no. 93.

21 Michele Girardi, *Giacomo Puccini. L'arte internazionale di un musicista italiano* (Venezia, Marsilio, 1995), p. 253.

22 [Ernest] Carbonne, *"Madame Butterfly" Tragédie Japonaise en trois actes de M. M. L. Illica et Giacosa. Traduction française de M.r Paul Ferrier Musique de M.r Giacomo Puccini Mise en Scène de M.r Albert Carré Rédigée par M.r Carbonne* (Paris, G.Ricordi & C.ie, s.d.).

23 Michaela Peterseil, "Die 'Disposizioni sceniche' des Verlags Ricordi ihre Publikation und ihr Zielpublikum," in *Studi verdiani* 12 (1997), p. 155.

24 Abbiati, IV:442, 444, 458–59.

25 *Carteggio Verdi-Boito*, ed. Mario Medici and Marcello Conati, with the collaboration of Marisa Casati (Parma, Istituto di studi verdiani, 1978), II:428.

26 *Carteggio Verdi-Boito*, I:213.

27 Abbiati, IV:458–59.

28 *Carteggio Verdi-Boito*, II:428.

29 Abbiati, IV:442, 471.

30 Josef-Horst Lederer, "Wie dieses Problem gelöst wurde ... war ein Helles Wunder." Verdi's Falstaff unter Gustav Mahler und Alfred Roller. Ein Beitrag zur Geschichte der Wiener Hofoper," in *La realizzazione scenica dello spettacolo verdiano*, ed. Pierluigi Petrobelli e Fabrizio Della Seta (Parma, Istituto nazionale di studi Verdiani, 1996), pp. 319–44

31 *"Sorgete! Ombre serene!". L'aspetto visivo dello spettacolo verdiano*, ed. Pierluigi Petrobelli, Marisa Di Gregorio Casati, and Olga Jesurum (Parma, Istituto nazionale di studi verdiani, 1994), pls. 70–77.

32 Abbiati, IV:442.

The Good, the Bad, and the Ugly: Character and Costume in the Theater of VERDI and PUCCINI

1 *Franco Abbiati, Giuseppe Verdi* (Milan, Ricordi, 1959), IV: 111.

2 Abbiati, *Verdi*, IV: 184.

3 Bardolfo [Eugenio Gara], writing in *Candido*, 17 January 1976.

4 Abbiati, IV: 483.

5 Giuseppe Valdengo, *Ho cantato con Toscanini* (Como, Cairoli Editore, 1962), p. 84.

6 E. Zorzi, writing in *L'Italia del Popolo*, 2-3 February 1896.

7 Tito Gobbi, *La mia vita* (Milan, Rusconi, 1985), p. 5.

8 Eugenio Gara, *Carteggi pucciniani* (Milan, Ricordi, 1958), p. 182.

9 Giuseppe Adami, *Epistolario* (Milan, Oscar Mondadori, 1982), p. 96.

10 *La lezione di Toscanini* (Atti del Convegno di studi toscaniniani al XXX Maggio musicale fiorentino), ed. Fedele D'Amico and Rosanna Paumgartner (Florence, Vallecchi Editore, 1970), p. 183.

11 *Epistolario*, p. 548.

Excursus: Opera as a Metaphor for Italy

1 Martin J. Gannon, *Understanding Global Cultures; Metaphorical Journeys Through 17 Countries* (Thousand Oaks, Ca, Sage Publications, 1994). In the second and third editions the number of countries treated from the point of view of their cultural metaphors was expanded to twenty-eight.

APPENDIX

BIOGRAPHIES

Thumbnail Sketches of the Protagonists of the Golden Century

Though this volume celebrates a full 200 years of Casa Ricordi, the dynasty of four consecutive generations of the Ricordi family that founded and directed the firm coincided almost exactly with a special era in opera history: the period known (in the felicitous term coined by the writer William Weaver) as the "Golden Century" of Italian opera. In that period of slightly over 100 years—from Rossini's *Il barbiere di Siviglia* (1816) to the posthumous performance of Puccini's *Turandot* (1926)—the popularity of Italian opera skyrocketed to unprecedented levels that found enthusiastic audiences around the world and cut across social strata. It was an era that witnessed the creation of enduring masterpieces that have remained in the opera repertory to this day.

Any attempt to list a representative sampling of the hundreds of superb creative talents who left their mark on that epoch is inevitably destined to inadequacy. Here below we offer brief sketches of a handful of the principal players of that amazing time from among those whose work and works are touched on in this book: the four Ricordis; the five composers who constitute the "pillars" of Italian opera repertory; and a few of the more influential librettists and designers.

The Ricordi dynasty

Giovanni Ricordi (1785–1853), ever tenacious and resourceful, was a musician whose body and soul were nourished by the acumen of an entrepreneur. When he founded Casa Ricordi in 1808 he had already acquired several years of experience as a theater violinist and copyist, an expanding archive of performing material, and a knowledge of music engraving. His combined objectives, music rental and publishing, were respectively innovative and avant-garde for their time, and they proved to be the foundation of an empire, a virtual monopoly in the field of theatrical music supply and derivative sales. One important consequence was his zealous commitment to copyright protection in the battle against misappropriation and piracy. Among his early "stable" of composers were Rossini, Bellini, Donizetti, and a promising young Verdi, who joined a catalog that would grow to become well more than 10,000 titles by the end of Giovanni's lifetime.

Tito I Ricordi (1811–1888) reaped the benefits of his father's resourceful business forays and expanded the activity into new cultural terrain, including publications of literature. Well educated and well traveled, he was friends with Schumann and Liszt and did much to support the dissemination of other musical genres beyond opera. As the inspiration behind the *Gazzetta musicale di Milano* he also helped establish the beginnings of systematic music criticism and research in Italy. Verdi considered him an instrumental force throughout the most productive (and profitable) years of his career.

Giulio Ricordi (1840–1912), the eldest of nine children, grew from a scrappy youth to become a veritable patron of the musical arts. An able composer and perceptive critic with a curriculum of charming compositions (as Jules Burgmein) and unrivaled editorial integrity, he would become a legendary name in the annals of music publishing. Giulio guided the company through its most glorious years spanning three generations of steadfast alliance: filial with Verdi, fraternal with Boito, and paternal with Puccini.

Tito II Ricordi (1865–1933), the last of the Ricordi dynasty to serve as director of the publishing house, was trained as an engineer but soon entered the firm alongside his father. His decided predilection for stage direction found fertile ground in the operas of Puccini, while his industrial ambitions were brisk and broad, with clear international designs. Impulsive and authoritative but also authoritarian, Tito left the helm of the company in 1919 after only seven years of turbulent navigation.

Composers

Gioachino Rossini (1792 – 1868), born into a musical family in Pesaro, wasted little time turning his well-trained talent to fine advantage, composing 39 operas in the space of little more than 25 years. His rapid rise to international fame and fortune was followed by early retirement from the stage, and he eventually became a permanent and influential fixture of Parisian artistic circles and generously championed young composers. Rossini's name generally conjures images of unmitigated delight in such comic operas as *Il barbiere di Siviglia* (1816), but his last opera,

Guillaume Tell (1829), is as great a contribution among many he made to the serious genre as well.

Gaetano Donizetti (1797–1848) received rigorous compositional training in his native Bergamo and was blessed with a facile and fluent vein of creativity that produced nearly 70 operas, including several with his own libretti. A singularly good-hearted and generous individual, he endured an often fickle fortune. Considered the first true exponent of Italian Romanticism, his innovative dramatic style would be the most powerful influence on Verdi. That eternal classics such as *L'elisir d'amore*, *Lucia di Lammermoor*, and *Don Pasquale* have remained in the repertory almost without interruption speaks worlds of his high place in the history of opera.

Vincenzo Bellini (1801–1835) died tragically young just as his fame was reaching impressive heights. Born in Catania of a musical family and trained in Naples, he composed just ten operas in as many years. A master of the Italian *bel canto* style and famed for his long and sensuous melodies, his influence even beyond Italian opera is apparent in the early works of Richard Wagner and the piano music of Frédéric Chopin. Among his enduring masterpieces are, *La sonnambula* and *Norma*.

Giuseppe Verdi (1813–1901), born of humble circumstances near Parma, received his music education there and in Milan. A legendary figure even during his own lifetime, he was a genuine man of the theater with a powerful sense of captivating melody and effective dramatic impact. Throughout his life he remained an ambassador of Italian values and tradition both on stage and off. The majority of his 28 operas occupy a prominent part of the repertory, many of them—*Rigoletto*, *La traviata*, *Il trovatore*, *Don Carlo*, *Aida*, *Otello*, and *Falstaff*—among the most beloved favorites of audiences the world over.

Giacomo Puccini (1858–1924) was born into a family of five generations of musicians in Lucca. Hints of inspiration surface in his youthful thirty-mile pilgrimage on foot to attend a performance of Verdi's *Aida*, or his fascination with Wagner and French opera while a student in Milan, but the wellspring of his language and style remained distinctly his own. His seamless sense of dramatic momentum, subtle melodic and harmonic invention, and superb orchestrational skill are timeless tools that allowed him to tap the universal vein of human empathy without sacrificing intellectual interest in the psychological portrayal of the characters. Puccini composed 12 operas, half of them, including *La bohème*, *Tosca*, and *Madama Butterfly*, among the most popular titles in the entire repertory.

Librettists

Felice Romani (1788–1865), the most famous Italian librettist of the 1820s and '30s and a dazzlingly prolific one, was the "house poet" for Milan's Teatro alla Scala, where he was required to provide six new librettos a year (his deadlines: 40 days for serious works, 60 days for comedies). A refined and elegant craftsman, over the span of his long career he provided texts for Rossini, Bellini (including *La sonnambula* and *Norma*), and Donizetti (including *Anna Bolena* and *L'elisir d'amore*), as well as one set to music by the young Verdi.

Salvadore Cammarano (1801–1852) is considered the greatest librettist of Italian opera of the Romantic era. A true "man of the theater," at Naples he would become, like Felice Romani in Milan, a professional "house poet"—part of the staff hired by the theater management. Among his expertly crafted and superbly "musical" texts are such immortal works as *Lucia di Lammermoor* for Donizetti and *Il trovatore* for Verdi.

Giuseppe Giacosa (1847–1906) was an author and playwright with a predilection for naturalism. As a librettist his most significant contributions were his three collaborative efforts with Luigi Illica for Puccini: *La bohème*, *Tosca*, and *Madama Butterfly*. Giacosa's strengths were predominantly lyrical, while Illica chiseled and shaped the appropriate verse structure. Nicknamed "Buddha" by Puccini for his corpulent girth and good humor, he was often the buffer in the many moments of dissension between the composer and his librettists.

Luigi Illica (1857–1919), a true "bohemian" in life as in art, began his career as a penniless writer in Milan. A man of "advanced views" he nonetheless had a fiery, confrontational character: he lost half an ear in a duel, served in World War I at age 60, and after the death of the mediating Giacosa would never work with Puccini again. After the three

BIOGRAPHIES

successful librettos written with Giacosa for Puccini he went on to write *Iris* for Pietro Mascagni and *Andrea Chénier* for Umberto Giordano.

Arrigo Boito (1842–1918) was a skilled composer (he wrote both the libretto and music of *Mefistofele* and *Nerone*) as well as a man of letters of uncommon gifts. A radical reformer of musical style in his youth and opponent of the "old style" of Verdi, he later became Verdi's most trusting and trustworthy librettist. His two Shakespeare-based librettos for Verdi, *Otello* and *Falstaff*, are considered among the most erudite and skillfully crafted texts in all of opera. Under the anagram pseudonym Tobia Gorrio he also penned the text for Amilcare Ponchielli's *La gioconda*.

Visual Artists

Alessandro Sanquirico (1777–1849) was the most important Italian scenographer of the early 19th century. After studying architecture with Giuseppe Piermarini—the architect of Milan's Teatro alla Scala—he began working in that theater as set designer from the start of the century through the première of Bellini's *Norma* (1831). Artistically he bridged the transition period between the elegance and majesty of Neoclassicism and the new aesthetics of Romanticism. The widely published lithographs and hand-colored etchings of his set designs influenced a generation of scenographers.

Adolf Hohenstein (1854–1928), after studying art in Vienna, was hired by Giulio Ricordi as the art director for the graphic-arts arm of the Milan publishing house, where he also served as a set and costume designer, collaborating on several opera productions including Verdi's *Falstaff* (1893) and all of Puccini's operas up through *Madama Butterfly* (1904). While at Ricordi he coordinated editorial promotion with designs for the covers of scores and librettos, postcards and publicity posters. A brilliant representative of the Art Nouveau style, his *affiche* for *La bohème* was the first of its kind for Italian opera, while those for *Tosca* and *Butterfly* are considered masterpieces of poster art.

Alfredo Edel (1856–1912), the most celebrated Italian costumier of his day, designed the costumes for more than 300 theatrical productions, including Verdi's revised *Simon Boccanegra*, *Don Carlo*, and *Otello*, and the famous ballet *Excelsior* by Marenco. He also worked at the Théâtre des Variétés and Comédie Française in Paris, and as a fashion designer and illustrator. Admired for his good taste and the originality of his designs, his specialty was coordinating the color and texture of a complete stage tableau.

SELECTED BIBLIOGRAPHY

The following list offers a selection of sources for further reading in the various areas discussed in this volume.

For a general overview of opera:

The Oxford Illustrated History of Opera. Edited by Roger Parker. Oxford: Oxford University Press, 1994.

Opera in Theory and Practice, Image and Myth. Edited by Lorenzo Bianconi and Giorgio Pestelli. Translated by Kenneth Chalmers and Mary Whittall. Chicago: University of Chicago Press, 2003.

On the five principal composers of the Italian "Golden Century":

Osborne, Richard. *Rossini.* New York: Cambridge University Press, 2007.

Ashbrook, William. *Donizetti and His Operas.* New York: Cambridge University Press, 1982.

Rosselli, John. *The Life of Bellini.* New York: Cambridge University Press, 1996.

Abbiati, Franco. *Giuseppe Verdi.* Milan: Ricordi, 1959.

Budden, Julian. *The Operas of Verdi.* Oxford: Oxford University Press, 1992.

Rosselli, John. *The Life of Verdi.* New York: Cambridge University Press, 2000.

Ashbrook, William. *The Operas of Puccini.* Ithaca: Cornell University Press, 1985.

Budden, Julian. *Puccini: His Life and Works.* Oxford: Oxford University Press, 2002.

Carteggi pucciniani. Edited by Eugenio Gara. Milan: Ricordi, 1955.

Girardi, Michele. *Puccini: His International Art.* Translated by Laura Basini. Chicago: University of Chicago Press, 1995.

Schickling, Dieter. *Giacomo Puccini. Biografie.* Stuttgart: Carus, 1989, new edition 2007.

All-in-one: Ashbrook, William, Julian Budden, Mosco Carner, Philip Gossett, Friedrich Lippman, Andrew Porter. *The New Grove Masters of Italian Opera: Rossini, Donizetti, Bellini, Verdi, Puccini.* New York, W.W. Norton, 1997.

On how a composer conceives and gives final shape to an opera, and how he may later return to revise it:

Gossett, Philip. *"Anna Bolena" and the Artistic Maturity of Gaetano Donizetti.* Oxford: Clarendon Press, 1985.

Parker, Roger. *Remaking the Song: Operatic Visions and Revisions from Handel to Berio.* Berkeley: University of California Press, 2006.

On some of the principal librettists, and on the composer-librettist interaction:

Ashbrook, William and Harold Powers. *Puccini's "Turandot": The End of the Great Tradition.* Princeton: Princeton University Press, 1991.

Black, John. *The Italian Romantic Libretto: A Study of Salvadore Cammarano.* Edinburgh: Edinburgh University Press, 1984.

Roccatagliati, Alessandro. *Felice Romani librettista.* Lucca: LIM, 1996.

The Verdi-Boito Correspondence. Edited by Marcello Conati and Mario Medici. Translated and annotated by William Weaver. Chicago: University of Chicago Press, 1994.

On scenography, costumes, and staging:

Biggi, Maria Ida, Maria Rosaria Corchia, and Mercedes Viale Ferrero. *Alessandro Sanquirico "il Rossini della pittura scenica."* Pesaro: Fondazione Gioachino Rossini, 2007.

Celeste Aida. Edited by Gabriele Dotto and Ilaria Narici. Milano: Ricordi, 2006.

APPENDIX

SELECTED BIBLIOGRAPHY

La scena di Puccini. Edited by Vittorio Fagone and Vittoria Crespi Morbio. Lucca: Edizioni Maria Pacini Fazzi, 2003.

Hepokoski, James A. and Mercedes Viale Ferrero. *"Otello" di Giuseppe Verdi.* Milano: Ricordi, 1990 (contains a reproduction of the *disposizione scenica*).

Opera on Stage. Edited by Lorenzo Bianconi and Giorgio Pestelli. Translated by Kate Singleton. Chicago: University Of Chicago Press, 2002.

Pigozzi, Marinella and David Rosen. *"Un ballo in maschera" di Giuseppe Verdi.* Milano: Ricordi, 2002 (contains a reproduction of the *disposizione scenica*).

La realizzazione scenica dello spettacolo verdiano. Atti del congresso internazionale di studi, Parma 28-30 settembre 1994. Edited by Pierluigi Petrobelli and Fabrizio Della Seta. Parma: Istituto nazionale di studi verdiani, 1996.

"Sorgete! Ombre serene!" L'aspetto visivo dello spettacolo verdiano. Edited by Pierluigi Petrobelli, Marisa Di Gregorio Casati, and Olga Jesurum. Parma: Istituto nazionale di studi verdiani, 1994.

Verdi in Performance. Edited by Alison Latham and Roger Parker. New York: Oxford University Press, 2001.

Viale Ferrero, Mercedes. *La scenografia della Scala nell'età neoclassica.* Milano: Il polifilo, 1983.

On Casa Ricordi:

Degrada, Francesco et. al. *Music, Musicians, and Publishing: 175 Years of Casa Ricordi.* Translated by Gabriele Dotto and Anna Herklotz. Milano: Ricordi, 1983.

Jensen, Luke. *Giuseppe Verdi & Giovanni Ricordi, with Notes on Francesco Lucca: From "Oberto" to "La traviata."* New York: Garland, 1989.

Sartori, Claudio. *Casa Ricordi 1808–1958.* Milano: Ricordi, 1958.

On the "business" of opera:

Opera Production and Its Resources. Edited by Lorenzo Bianconi and Giorgio Pestelli. Translated by Lydia Cochrane. Chicago: University of Chicago Press, 1998.

Rosselli, John. *The Opera Industry in Italy from Cimarosa to Verdi: The Role of the Impresario.* New York: Cambridge University Press, 1984.

On preparing and performing critical editions of 19th-century opera:

Gossett, Philip. *Divas and Scholars: Performing Italian Opera.* Chicago: University of Chicago Press, 2006.

On modern Italian opera:

Fearn, Raymond. *Italian Opera Since 1945.* Oxford: Routledge, 1998.

CONTRIBUTORS

Vittoria Crespi Morbio, an expert on the relationship between the figurative arts and opera, has curated exhibitions in Milan, Spoleto, Lucca, Brescia, Amsterdam, Tokyo, and New York. The author of numerous monographs on designers such as Pier Luigi Pizzi, Franca Squarciapino, Ezio Frigerio, Marcello Dudovich, Leopoldo Metlicovitz, Lila De Nobili, and Franco Zeffirelli, she recently edited *Maria Callas, gli anni della Scala* (Milan, Allemandi, 2007).

Gabriele Dotto was on the editorial staff of Casa Ricordi for almost two decades, ultimately becoming director of publishing and, at the same time, director of its archive. The co-general editor (with R. Parker) of the Donizetti critical edition and general editor of the Puccini critical edition, he has edited operas by Rossini and Donizetti and published essays on late 19th- and 20th-century Italian opera.

Jean-Jacques Nattiez, professor of musicology at the University of Montreal, is specialized in Wagner and has written on issues of opera as a genre, opera's esthetics, and the problems of staging. General editor of the five-volume *Enciclopedia della musica* (Milan, Einaudi, 2001–05), among his publications are *Tétralogies: Wagner, Boulez, Chéreau* (Paris, Bourgois, 1983), *Wagner androgyne* (Paris, Bourgois, 1990), and a novel, *Opera* (Montreal, Leméac, 1997).

Roger Parker is professor of music at King's College London. He has written widely on aspects of Italian opera and has published critical editions of operas by Verdi and Donizetti. The co-general editor (with G. Dotto) of the Donizetti critical edition, his most recent book is *Remaking the Song: Operatic Visions and Revisions from Handel to Berio* (Berkeley, University of California Press, 2006).

Pierluigi Petrobelli, director of the Istituto nazionale di studi verdiani (Parma) and professor emeritus at the University "La sapienza" of Rome, has published over 200 essays with special emphasis on Mozart and 19th-century opera (especially Verdi and Bellini). Co-editor (with W. Rehm) of the critical edition of Mozart's *Il re pastore*, he published *Music in the Theater: Essays on Verdi and Other Composers* (Princeton, Princeton University Press, 1994).

Severino Salvemini, professor of organization theory at the Bocconi University of Milan, has written extensively on cultural management and cultural industries. Among his publications in this field are *Il cinema italiano. Imprenditorialità, efficienza e innovazione* (Rome, Anec, 1992), *Tra cultura e mercato* (Bologna, il Mulino, 1992), *Artwork & Network* (Milan, Egea, 2001), *La città creativa* (id., 2005), and *È tutto un altro film* (id., 2007).

Dieter Schickling is a member of the board of directors and the advisory board of the "Centro studi Giacomo Puccini" (Lucca) and serves on the editorial board of the complete works of Puccini. Author of numerous articles on the composer, he published *Giacomo Puccini: Catalogue of the Works* (Kassel, Bärenreiter, 2003) and *Giacomo Puccini. Biografie* (Stuttgart, Carus, 1989, new edition 2007).

Mercedes Viale Ferrero has curated several exhibitions on the visual aspects of opera and published essays and books on the subject, including *La scenografia della Scala nell'età neoclassica* (Milan, Il polifilo, 1983), *"Otello" di Giuseppe Verdi* (with J.A. Hepokoski; Milan, Ricordi, 1990), and, most recently, *Alessandro Sanquirico "il Rossini della pittura scenica"* (with M.I. Biggi and M.R. Corchia; Pesaro, Fondazione Rossini, 2007).

Luca Zoppelli, professor of musicology at the University of Fribourg (Switzerland), has written on the relationship between rhetoric and music, on 18th-century music aesthetics, and 19th-century opera. Co-general editor (with F. della Seta and A. Roccatagliati) of the critical edition of Vincenzo Bellini, he is preparing an edition of Donizetti's *Maria di Rohan*. Among his publications is *L'opera come racconto. Modi narrativi nel teatro musicale dell'Ottocento* (Venice, Marsilio, 1994).

CREDITS

This catalog is published on the occasion of

That's Opera
200 Years of Italian Music

World Tour Exhibition

Under the Patronage of

H.E. The President of the Italian Republic

Ministero per i Beni e le Attività Culturali

Comune di Milano

With the Support of

Comitato Nazionale per le Celebrazioni del Bicentenario della Fondazione di Casa Ricordi 1808-2008

Initiator

Ricordi & C. SpA, Milan

Tino Cennamo
Managing Director, Ricordi & C. SpA,
and President, Comitato Nazionale Ricordi

Presenter

Bertelsmann AG, Gütersloh

Thomas Rabe
Chief Financial Officer and Member of the Board,
Bertelsmann AG, and President, Ricordi & C. SpA

Denise Abel
Max Dressendörfer
Helen Müller

Project Management

Steve de Bonvoisin, Bertelsmann AG

Communication and Marketing Consultant

Jasmine Borhan, Munich

Touring Exhibition

Exhibition Curator
Jean-Jacques Nattiez
Professeur de Musicologie,
Université de Montréal

Advisory Board

Gabriele Dotto
Director, Michigan State University Press

Roger Parker
Thurston Dart Professor of Music, King's College London

Pierluigi Petrobelli
Director, Istituto nazionale di studi verdiani, Parma

Dieter Schickling
Board Member, Centro studi Giacomo Puccini, Lucca

Ricordi & C. SpA, Milan

Iolanda Argentino
Francesca Calciolari
Maria-Pia Ferraris
Pierluigi Ledda

Institutional Relations

Kikka Ricchio, Musicart Srl

Main Lender

Ricordi & C. SpA, Milan

Lenders

Arnoldo Pomodoro, Milan

Ermanno Olmi, Milan

Biblioteca Nazionale Braidense, Milan

Museo Teatrale alla Scala, Milan

Archivio Fotografico Teatro alla Scala, Milan

Claudio Ricordi

Istituto Luce

Civiche Raccolte d'Arte Applicata ed Incisioni, Milan

Museo Luigi Illica, Piacenza

Sony BMG Entertainment Italy

Fondazione Corriere della Sera

Civica Raccolta delle Stampe Achille Bertarelli, Milan

Sony BMG Entertainment, New York

Universal Music MGB Publications, Italy

Staatstheater Stuttgart

La Monnaie, Brussels

Bayerische Staatsoper, München

bpk / **Staatsbibliothek zu Berlin - Preußischer Kulturbesitz**

Beinecke Rare Book and Manuscript Library, Yale University

General Contractor and Realization

atelier brückner gmbh, Stuttgart

Concept & Design

Creative Director
Uwe R. Brückner

Managing Director
Shirin Frangoul-Brückner

Project Management
Birgit Kadatz

Design Team
Adriana Castro
Carina Ernst
Frank Forell
Sibylla Gottschall
Anja Heinzel
Maria Millan
Jonas Togler
Tatjana Triebelhorn

Consultant for Stage Design and Costume
Ulrike Schlemm
Werner Pick

Media Planning
medienprojekt p2 GmbH, Stuttgart
Matthias de Ponte

Light Design and Planning
LDE Belzner Holmes, Heidelberg
Andrew Holmes

CREDITS

Exhibition Production

Production & Logistics
Nüssli (Schweiz) AG, Hüttwilen
Daniel Günther
Stefan Stocker
Patrick Wallain
Tilmann Hecht

Media Design & Production
jangled nerves GmbH, Stuttgart
Thomas Hundt
Gesina Geiger
Thomas Lauterbach

Personal Digital Assistant
Nous Wissensmanagement Gmbh, Wien
Alexander Stickelberger

Theatre Painting
Peter Böck

Tailoring
Frauke Ollmann

Content & Research, Tour Organization

Institut für Kulturaustausch, Tübingen

Managing Director
Otto Letze

Content
Maria Espinosa
Sandra Sara Motta

Tour Organization
Meike Niepelt
Roland Oberzig

Texts Children's Level
Urbanes Texten, Berlin
Stephanie Jäckel

Proof Reading
Deutsch-Amerikanisches Institut Tübingen
Barig Nalbantian

Translations
Intra, Stuttgart

Communication & Media Planning

Dorten GmbH, Stuttgart

Concept
Tommi Brem
Oliver Schmid

Project Management
Verena Schiml

Creative Direction
Jörg Bauer

Art Direction and Design
Dorten Bauer
Bjørn Küenzlen
Anthony Lynch

Media Partner

RTL-TVi

Sponsor

JPMORGAN

EXHIBITION CATALOG EDITOR

Gabriele Dotto
Director, Michigan State University Press

WITH A SPECIAL INTRODUCTION BY
Plácido Domingo

CONTRIBUTORS

Vittoria Crespi Morbio
Milan

Gabriele Dotto
Director, Michigan State University Press

Jean-Jacques Nattiez
Professeur de Musicologie, Université de Montréal

Roger Parker
Thurston Dart Professor of Music, King's College London

Pierluigi Petrobelli
Director, Istituto nazionale di studi Verdiani, Parma

Severino Salvemini
Professore di Organizzazione aziendale,
Università Bocconi, Milan

Dieter Schickling
Board Member, Centro studi Giacomo Puccini, Lucca

Mercedes Viale Ferrero
Turin

Luca Zoppelli
Professeur de Musicologie, Université de Fribourg,
Switzerland

EDITORIAL OFFICE

INSTITUT FÜR KULTURAUSTAUSCH
Otto Letze
Maria Espinosa
Sandra Sara Motta
Meike Niepelt

RICORDI & C. SPA
Francesca Calciolari
Maria-Pia Ferraris
Pierluigi Ledda

LAYOUT & DESIGN

DORTEN BAUER
Jörg Bauer, Creative Director
Bjørn Küenzlen
Anthony Lynch

ACKNOWLEDGMENTS

We would like to extend our thanks to the advisors, lenders, directors and curators, and the following people who have contributed to the organization of the exhibition and the preparation of the catalog in many different ways:

Marie Gofette, Brussels
Camillo Ricordi
Direzione Generale dei Beni Librari e Istituti Culturali
Teatro alla Scala, Milan
MITO Festival Internazionale della Musica, Milan
Soprintendenza Archivistica per la Lombardia
Philipp Nedel, b-sharp, music and media solutions

IMPRINT

FRONTISPIECE: A.T. Schaefer, Stuttgart

IMAGE CREDITS
© for the reproduced works unless otherwise noted:
RICORDI & C. SPA, MILAN

Page 64/65: Autograph musical sketch *La traviata* by Giuseppe Verdi · Used by kind permission of the Verdi heirs.

Page 91: Photograph of the set design "La Barrière d'Enfer" by Lucien Jusseaume · Bibliothèque nationale de France, Paris. Used by permission.

PRESTEL VERLAG
Königinstrasse 9
80539 Munich
Tel. +49 (0)89 24 29 08-300
Fax +49 (0)89 24 29 08-335

PRESTEL PUBLISHING LTD.
4 Bloomsbury Place
London WC1A 2QA
Tel. +44 (0)20 73 23-50 04
Fax +44 (0)20 76 36-80 04

PRESTEL PUBLISHING
900 Broadway, Suite 603
New York, N.Y. 10003
Tel. +1 (212) 995-27 20
Fax +1 (212) 995-27 33

WWW.PRESTEL.COM

Prestel books are available worldwide. Please contact your nearest bookseller or one of the above addresses for information concerning your local distributor.
The Library of Congress Cataloguing-in-Publication data is available.

British Library Cataloguing-in-Publication Data: a catalog record for this book is available from the British Library.
The Deutsche Bibliothek holds a record of this publication in the Deutsche Nationalbibliografie; detailed bibliographical data can be found under: http://dnb.ddb.de

PROJECT MANAGEMENT BY Gabriele Ebbecke

EDITORIAL DIRECTION BY Doris Hansmann, Büro für Lektorat & Producing, Köln

TRANSLATED FROM THE ITALIAN BY David Radzinowicz (Crespi Morbio, Fallace, Moratti, Petrobelli, Salvemini, Zoppelli), Sarah Kane (Viale Ferrero) and Anna Herklotz (Domingo)

TRANSLATED FROM THE FRENCH BY David Radzinowicz (Nattiez)

TRANSLATED FROM THE GERMAN BY Cynthia Hall (Schickling)

PROOFREADING BY Cynthia Hall

DESIGN AND LAYOUT BY Dorten GmbH/Dorten Bauer, Stuttgart

PRODUCTION BY Simone Zeeb

ORIGINATION BY Undercover GmbH, Stuttgart

PRINTED AND BOUND BY TBB, Banská Bystrica

PRINTED IN Slovakia on acid-free paper

ISBN 978-3-7913-4133-0 (TRADE EDITION ENGLISH)
ISBN 978-3-7913-6204-5 (MUSEUM EDITION ENGLISH)
ISBN 978-3-7913-6205-2 (MUSEUM EDITION FRENCH)